Willia

WHO ARE YOU?

**Answering questions about
You, Me and God**

CF4•K

10 9 8 7 6 5 4 3 2 1
Copyright © William Edgar 2019

paperback ISBN 978-1-5271-0340-5
epub ISBN 978-1-5271-0379-5
mobi ISBN 978-1-5271-0380-1

Published in 2019
by
Christian Focus Publications, Ltd.
Geanies House, Fearn,
Ross-shire, IV20 1TW, Scotland.
www.christianfocus.com

Cover design by Tom Barnard

Printed and bound by
Bell & Bell, Glasgow

Contents

Dedication

To Peter and Sandra Moore,
with deepest gratitude.

Who am I?

AN IDENTITY WOULD SEEM TO BE ARRIVED AT BY THE WAY IN WHICH
THE PERSON FACES AND USES HIS EXPERIENCE.
(JAMES BALDWIN)

When I was a teenager, as it was for most young people my age, very few things were settled. Oh, I had a solid and loving family. My parents had endured the Great Depression and World War II, and communicated the value of hard work and respect for Western civilization to my brother and me. I was sent away to boarding school, which was the tradition in our family. The curriculum was quite standard, having been shaped by decades of commitment to the importance for any educated person of mathematics, literature, history, and the like. Sports were stressed a good deal, which suited me well, as I was a decent athlete and enjoyed the exertion and the competition. There was obligatory chapel, which most of us endured without much personal faith. The school was called a preparatory school, as the basic goal for every student was getting admitted to college (as Americans call university).

In that way everything was, more or less, preset. If we didn't study hard enough, we were threatened with not going to college. If we excelled on the athletic field we might be recruited by one of these colleges to play on their teams, which in America meant a good deal. At the same time, for me, something was missing. Was getting into college such a cure-all? Was that all there was to life? When I asked my parents or some of the teachers (called 'masters') why we were doing all this, remarkably little substance was offered, at least in my judgment. They talked vaguely about being prepared for life, whatever that meant.

I was really searching. With a couple of friends, I began to read the Existentialists. Albert Camus was my favorite. Although he was pessimistic, in a number of ways, he had a profound sense of the worth and dignity of every human being. Above all he cared about justice, something I cared about more and more at my young age. When I did arrive in college I studied as much French literature as I could, as well as other guides in the quest for justice.

I might not have put it quite this way at the time, but I was really trying to find out who I was. Under the guidance of a kindly university instructor, and a number of other influences, I did find out. I discovered the Christian faith. Today, I would say, it discovered me! On the following pages I wish to introduce the reader to some of the ways my new-found identity has given meaning to several of my inquiries, including my quest for justice. I want to respond to the many questions I have either had for myself or received from others about the Christian religion. But first, a few thoughts about the issue of identity.

You may know that the Christian faith has played a large part in shaping our Western idea of who the human person is. It took a while, but over the centuries, a truly Christian understanding of the nature of human beings replaced both ancient Greek and pagan notions. Particularly from the Protestant Reformation onward, human identity was considered to be who we are before God himself. To put it in biblical language, we are made after God's own image. What this means is that each person, you and I, have our primary identity as godlike beings, capable of loving, thinking, working, and worshiping.

This has all kinds of implications. Today we take it for granted that we may choose our profession, choose our spouse, and choose to live in a certain place. There was a time when all of those were fixed. Children took over the family business, their marriages were arranged, and it was rare to move away from where one had grown up. Because of the impact of the Christian faith it gradually occurred to people that their identity was more than in their social group or their lot in life. It was in their primary relationship to God. The much maligned group, known as the Puritans, helped us refine this understanding by emphasizing human calling before God. As some of them used to put it, their life was lived first and foremost before an 'audience of one,' namely, God. What a contrast to what we experience today when so much of life is based on performance, or achievement, and this before several audiences, such as parents, teachers, or even the celebrities we try to emulate. There is a place for some of that, but the great breakthrough in the Christian faith is its focus on the primary, vertical relationship with the Lord God.

The Sovereign Self

For you have died, and your life is hidden with Christ in God. When Christ who is your life appears, then you also will appear with him in glory (Colossians 3:3-4).

The pendulum swung to the other side. But has it not swung too far? Today the individual is considered sovereign, and the vertical relationship has been eclipsed. Indeed, instead of the audience of one, the entire audience is now the self. We have moved from being godlike to behaving as though we were gods. One hears it in popular speech. 'You owe it to yourself,' 'take control of your finances,' 'you need a good self-image.' Recently, my wife and I have attended several graduation ceremonies. The typical message from speakers and administrators is similar: 'be honest to yourself,' 'follow your heart,' 'listen to your inner child,' and the like. The problem with this approach is that it sounds marvelous, until you realize it cannot be done.

When I was a Sixth Former (12th grader) about to graduate, if someone had told me to follow my dreams it would have sounded lovely, until it would dawn on me that my dreams were not coherent. I had no idea what I wanted to be or do. I had this vague sense that I cared about justice, but the idea had no foundation. Consequently, I had no foundation upon which to construct meaningful decisions. Of course, I had many interests, including football (soccer), French literature, music, and so forth. Indeed, I decided to read music at university. But at the deepest level, I really had no idea who I was. In the more traditional societies, there was a fairly low bar. Your future might have been confining, but it wasn't hard to decide what you were going to do. However, today we have affirmed the sovereign self. Despite all the talk of following your heart, very few people know what their heart is telling them. The sovereign self is simply incapable of giving guidance.

One place the pressure is coming from, ironically, is identity politics. That is, we define who we are quite narrowly, in terms of an ideology. Perhaps we are liberal. Or conservative. Perhaps we have same-sex attraction. Maybe we are heterosexual. What popular culture tells us is to follow those impulses, because they tell us who we are. But do they? Important as it is within a proper context, do we really want to affirm that our sexual preference is the key to who we are? A friend of mine recently had a conversation with a relative who is a lesbian. She announced to him that he couldn't love her because he denied her basic identity. My friend tried to explain that he did love her, first, because she was family, and second, simply because she was made after God's image. He disagrees with her sexual orientation and yet he still loves her as a sister. He tried to persuade her that her basic identity was not her sexual orientation but her being one of God's creatures. Then the idea came to him. He asked her if she loved him. In fact, she did and was glad to say so. Well, then, he told her, 'I know you disagree with my Christian faith. I claim my identity to be in Jesus Christ. But that doesn't stop you from loving me. Can't I also love you without embracing your sexual orientation?' That gave her great pause.

My Career

FOR ME TO LIVE IS CHRIST AND TO DIE IS GAIN (PHILIPPIANS 1:21).

One of the most common views of identity today is getting the right job. Years ago, my wife and I were moving our daughter into her dormitory room at university. There we met her new roommates. I well remember the conversation I had with one young woman. I asked what her aspirations were. Without hesitation she replied, to get into a good graduate school so I can qualify for a good job, then everything else should work out fine. I did not want to lecture her, and I partly approved her serious motivations. But I eventually tried to encourage her to look at the bigger picture. Why not enjoy these four unique years with so many resources at your disposal? Don't you know how many people have jobs and are not satisfied? Today, several years later, job retention is famously elusive to young people. In North America, the average university graduate changes work at least six times in the first decade. It is even considered a weakness to stay too long in one place. It's a two-way street, since many companies make few attempts to retain their younger employees.

Not only lack of commitment on both sides, but also disillusionment strikes hard. Many employees begin with great enthusiasm but soon find problems at work. They may have difficulty with a superior. They may be disappointed in the culture of the workplace. They may end the day simply unfulfilled. Of course, these are real problems, and many places of employment, indeed most, are far from perfect. But if your primary identity is the job, disenchantment lurks at the door.

Now, if your primary identity is from the audience of one, then you can have the best of both worlds. First, when you know God loves you and has made you after his own image in order that you may know him and walk with him, then your identity is unshakable. Second, then everything else can fall into place, the job, your family, your social status, your money … Here is a prayer I say every Monday morning before I go out to work. Notice it is both deeply meaningful and deeply realistic:

O God, at whose word man goeth forth to his work and to his labor until the evening; Be merciful to all whose duties are difficult or burdensome, and comfort them concerning their toil. Shield from bodily accident and harm the workmen at their work. Protect their efforts of sober and honest industry and suffer not the hire of laborers to be kept back by fraud. Incline the heart of employers and of those whom they employ to mutual forbearance, fairness and good-will. Give the spirit of governance and of a sound mind to all in places of authority. Bless all those who labor in works of mercy or in schools of good learning. Care for all aged persons, and all little children, the sick and the afflicted, and those who travel by land or by sea. Remember all those who by reason of weakness are overtasked, or because of poverty are forgotten. Let the sorrowful sighing of the prisoners come before thee; and according to the greatness of thy power, preserve thou those that are appointed to die. Give ear to our prayer,

O merciful and gracious Father, for the love of thy dear Son, our Savior Jesus Christ. Amen.[1]

Good but not Absolute

AND I WILL GIVE HIM A WHITE STONE, WITH A NEW NAME WRITTEN ON THE STONE (REVELATION 2:17).

Finding your identity does not mean getting rid of all your ambitions. Nor does it mean becoming 'spiritual' in the wrong way, that is, to be 'so heavenly minded as to be no earthly good,' as the expression goes. There is a tradition in the history of the church called mysticism. There are many varieties of mysticism, but most have in common a disdain for the world, and a gaze into the heavens that prizes intangible things over this-worldly living. It's an important balance to keep. The present world will not last. The world to come is the more permanent place. And yet this view should not lure us away from today's earthly tasks.

Here is an example from the New Testament. In his magnificently constructed letter to the Ephesians the apostle Paul describes the Christian life as one of blessedness, that is, of great joy in Jesus Christ (Ephesians 1:3). He declares God's purposes in us to be 'to the praise of his glorious grace' (1:6). This

1. John Heyl Vincent, *The Church at Home* (New York: The Christian Herald, 1904) p. 311.

language is about our existence being for the purpose of worshiping God. The language could not be more spiritual. The entire first half of this letter piles on the many dimensions of God's grace and mercy to us. Then, without leaving off these thoughts, the apostle focuses on application. Among other issues in the Christian life, Paul discusses money. It's brief but to the point:

> Let the thief no longer steal, but rather let him labor, doing honest work with his own hands, so that he might have something to share with anyone in need (Ephesians 4:28).

From the lofty heights of God's praise, we move to the need to reform the way we handle our finances. Stealing is not only the devious burglar who breaks into a home and makes off with the silver. It can be cheating on taxes, not sharing gratuities, siphoning fuel from another car, plagiarizing examination answers, and so forth. Even desiring something we shouldn't have is a form of theft. So, the apostle says that now that we are in Christ and have the power to change, we must desist from thieving. However, the gospel never stops at the negative. It always goes on to replace what is forbidden with what is now commended.

Paul says two things. First, we must work with our own hands. Manual labor is an important form of work, but today it is hardly the only form. There is a great variety of legitimate work we may engage in, from desk jobs to sales to scholarship to athletics, and much more. When he says to do it with our own hands he means the work must be our own, not done illegitimately. This, among other things, is a way to provide for oneself and one's family, before the 'audience of one'. But then second, he says to take some of the gain and give it to the needy. The whole subject of poverty relief is a large and complex one. But the principle is that we ought to do it.

How does this relate to identity? Because our human person is meant to be lived not only before God, who sees all, but in the light of Jesus Christ, who so loved us that 'though he was rich, yet for your sake he became poor, so that you by his poverty might become rich' (2 Corinthians 8:9). The great appeal of the gospel is that it gives us a new identity, one that is in continuity with our particular selves, yet makes us new persons. Our new self begins here in this life and then in the life to come will be raised up to enjoy fellowship with God forever. Paul in another place says that 'if anyone is in Christ he is a new creation' (2 Corinthians 5:17). That is true both now, even though we are still in our old frail bodies, and in the life to come when we will be made fully whole. C. S. Lewis puts this beautifully:

> The more we let God take us over, the more truly ourselves we become – because He made us. He invented us. He invented all the different people that you and I were intended to be ... It is when I turn to Christ, when I give myself up to His personality, that I first begin to have a real personality of my own.[2]

Discussion Questions:

1. Describe your own search for identity. What is it like? Where do you go for answers?

2. Do you feel there is too much pressure on you or your friends as individuals to make career choices at an early age?

3. Is work an over-rated value? Should we worry about unemployment? What are we to do if the perfect job does not show up for us? How should work be connected to our identity?

---

2. C.S. Lewis, *Mere Christianity* (New York: Touchstone – Simon & Schuster, 1996), p. 190.

Only one Way?

A COMMON MISTAKE WE MAKE IS THAT WE LOOK FOR GOD IN PLACES WHERE WE OURSELVES WISH TO FIND HIM (CHRIS JAMI).

When I was a child, I dreamed a good deal, as many children do. One of my recurrent dreams was being in a forest, or somewhere on a warm plain, but lost. Often, though these places were beautiful, I would feel rather desperate and frustrated at not finding the path home. Only when I woke up did I find a measure of relief. The apostle Paul (who wrote many of the letters in the New Testament) uses a similar image to describe how humanity is searching for the truth. He tells an Athenian audience that God made all of humanity and set all people in specific locations all over the earth, 'that they might feel their way toward him and find him' (Acts 17:27). The Greek word he uses for to 'feel their way' means something like seeking after the signs for a person or a thing. We know there is an answer, but we cannot find it. It communicates the same sense of trying to find a way out without total success.

What does the search for God look like in our times? Well, many are certainly feeling their way, searching for truth. My wife's grandmother, Barbara Morgan, was a considerable American philosopher. She wrote a book titled, Man's Restless Search.[1] Her thesis is that if we want to be happier we shall have to search with our spirits for some mystical beings, such as God. When we do, we should find fulfillment. She is not certain about the nature of such a being but affirms that the search itself is enough, for all religions are the same in the end. This is a common view. The search is better than the goal.

Many people believe that most or all the world's religions are basically the same. Jeffrey Moses, for example, affirms that one can indeed identify a common denominator in world religions. It is oneness.[2] The basic thesis of the book is that whatever the

1. Barbara Spofford Morgan, *Man's Restless Search*, New York: Harper & Bros, 1949.

2. Jeffrey Moses, *Oneness: Great Principles Shared by All Religions*, New York: Random House, 2002.

differences in expression, all the religions aspire to a common goal, helping humanity to live together through common moral imperatives. These are: the golden rule, love thy neighbor, honor thy father and mother, speak truth, it is more blessed to give than receive, and similar commandments. In this way, there is one set of things in common. The author then goes through many different scriptures from the different religions and quotes many so-called great masters and finds nearly identical adages in all of them.

All of this sounds lovely, until we ask a few basic questions. The first is how do we know the search is enough? How can Barbara Morgan be so sure that the journey is better than the goal? What if the search leads to a dead end? Her idea is that the human spirit is a rich enough residue of worthwhile resources so that we do not really have to affirm one religion over another. But can our souls bear the weight of such responsibility? And are we all good enough so that we can be trusted in our quest?

The second is whether the world religions really do teach the same things. Every single religion? Really? On what basis does Jeffrey Moses make his selection of the great religions and the great teachers? His list includes Christianity, Buddhism, Islam, Confucianism and a few others. He does not mention some of the more violent religions which practice conquest, widow-burning, the abandonment of baby girls, etc. Nor does he explain exactly why we should agree that these lofty principles are good ones. He assumes his own authority, without stating his premises. What the author never divulges is that his own views are shaped by the Enlightenment of the eighteenth century. Basically, the Enlightenment taught that if we trust in our reason, and if we are allowed enough freedom to practice reasonable values, then the world should improve. But this approach has significant problems. How do we know what is reasonable and what is not, unless we have a higher authority to judge by? And can the disasters of the past hundred years be accounted for merely because the rules of reason were not applied? The philosopher Friedrich Nietzsche clearly demonstrated that power, more than reason, drives human activity.

The question really is, do human beings possess the power to take the journey suggested by Morgan or to practice the love prescribed by Jeffrey Moses? Moses tells us that when our ability to love others is put to the test, 'Acts of faith, prayer, and deep meditation provide us with the strength that allows love for others to become an abiding part of our lives, of our beings.'[3] But can this possibly be true? Are there not times in life when such a test is simply too hard? Do we not need much more than religious methods? We need greater power. And we need some answers.

What about Different Religions?

AND HE MADE FROM ONE MAN EVERY NATION OF MANKIND... THAT THEY SHOULD SEEK GOD, IN THE HOPE THAT THEY MIGHT FEEL THEIR WAY TOWARD HIM AND FIND HIM. (ACTS 17:26-27)

During his remarks to the Athenians, the apostle goes on to say that, ironically, God is not far from each person, and that, indeed, we live and move and have our being in God, and we are his offspring (Acts 17:27-28). He employs a couple of quotes from local poets. So, Paul obviously thinks there are insights, important ones, in the different religions. While he is sharply critical of them, at one level, he is willing to acknowledge their wisdom at another.

That is a good model for us. There are great insights in some of the world religions. Even in the pop religion of our time, which wants to be spiritual without being religious, and wants to practice believing without belonging, there are deep intuitions. One of the daunting features of world religions is their

---

3. *Oneness*, p. 9.

great diversity. Even those who claim to be without any faith, or to be entirely skeptical, exhibit certain patterns that are fairly called religious. Are there any patterns at all? What do they really have in common? Without accepting Jeffrey Moses' categories I believe we can find shapes which give us important clues to what the apostle is saying about humanity's quest.[4]

To begin with, many adherents to non-Christian religions have a strong awareness of the inter-connectedness of all things. This is a most important insight. Thich Nhat Hahn, the Vietnamese Zen Buddhist, has coined the term interbeing to signify that the human self is connected at many levels with the rest of the world. Roman Catholic mystic Thomas Merton was quite taken by this concept.[5] The ancient religions of India, from which Zen comes, are unusually sensitive to the relationship of all living beings. This is true of ancient Chinese thought as well. We recently witnessed a total eclipse of the sun in North America. The reporters went around to

4. In what follows, I have been guided in part by the twentieth century missiologist J. H. Bavinck (1895-1964). See his writings on religious consciousness in *The J. H. Bavinck Reader*, eds. John Bolt, James D Bratt & Paul Visser, Grand Rapids: Eerdmans, 2013, pp. 145-299.

5. See Robert H. King, *Thomas Merton and Thich Nhat Hanh: Engaged Spirituality in an Age of Globalization,* London & New York: Continuum, 2001.

several places where it could be observed, wearing the right eyeglasses. Several people interviewed said they suddenly felt connected with the universe! If you are a Christian reading these lines your antennae will rightly go up: is this not to confuse the Creator with the creature? And are we not made after God's own image and thus carry royal blood in our veins? And you would be right. Yet at the same time we don't want to miss the great value of the sense of connectedness. Not only does it give us a greater awareness of the whole, but also of our own fragility. Scholar J. H. Bavinck comments: 'The inexpressible majesty of the totality is reflected in the stillness of the heart, just like the unbounded enormity of the heavens is reflected in the dewdrop clinging to the flower.'[6] Surely the apostle Paul was thinking of this sort of insight when quoting the two poets at Athens.

A second kind of awareness found in non-Christian religions is the notion of ethical standards. In my own conversations with unbelievers I have never encountered a person who is altogether devoid of a moral sense. Sometimes it is nearly inarticulate. When this is the case I usually try to find examples that will jolt them into either praise or perhaps

6. *The J. H. Bavinck Reader*, p. 162.

moral outrage. When I was a school teacher, I remember being frustrated at one young person's seeming inability to accept right and wrong. Every time we argued, he would say that such and such a sentiment was merely social convention. Until one day the subject of cruelty to animals came up. That was 'absolutely wrong', he had to admit. It may not seem like much, in a world where there is so much cruelty to people, but it was the open door to further conversations about human moral sense in this young man.

In the great religions of the world there is often a teaching about a cosmic order. In ancient India it was known as the Rita. In China it was called the Tao (pronounced Dao, from which we get Daoism). Everything is ruled by this cosmic order, your place in society, your moral standards, the rulings of the potentate, etc. In ancient Western tradition the great philosopher Plato thought everything to be ruled by the supreme good. Only by conforming to the universal good could a human being hope to live a harmonious life. Again, if you are a Christian reading this text, you will rightly say, there is no impersonal cosmic order, only the true God who rules according to his great wisdom. This is quite true. Yet the very fact that everyone has a moral sense is a pointer to the true God. Everyone knows, deep down, that there is right and there is wrong, and most people somehow know that their actions and even their thoughts will be judged one day. This is a powerful testimony to God's ultimate moral authority over all mankind. We often hear someone remark, 'He'll have a lot to answer for,' or the like.

Let me mention one other manifestation of religious awareness. It is that there is something quite wrong with our world, and we stand in need of deliverance. The great religions I have studied all have a deep sense of the grim reality of death. With remarkable diversity of expression we find the same themes in almost every faith: we were originally in paradise, then some horrible catastrophe took place spoiling it for us, and finally there is a way out. In India, it was believed that we have fallen into samsara, or 'wandering'. We are held captive by our senses, or by the sense of our individual significance. What we need is Moksha, inner deliverance, becoming detached from our limitations. In a word, we need freedom. The Christian can agree that we need freedom, not from captivity to our senses, but rather from sin, which is a moral turning against God. But the insights from Hinduism and other religions are not altogether erroneous.

Enough Ignorance

HOW LONG WILL YOU GO LIMPING BETWEEN TWO OPINIONS?
(1 KINGS 18:21)

We might be tempted at this point to say people have got many things right, so let's help them complete the picture. That is the opposite of what Paul does in Athens or anywhere else. Although he quotes the local poets approvingly, he also engages in a devastating critique of the Athenians' religion. He tells them their altars are shams, and that their view of moral responsibility is shallow. He counters with a speech about God the creator who is not manipulated by people, but who determines mankind's ways. And he tells them something quite startling. All of their thoughts and actions, indeed the whole world will be judged by this God. In a momentous conclusion he tells them the proof of all this is Christ's resurrection. In view of the future judgment and resurrection, they should repent, that is, engage in a personal revolution, coming to the true God in faith. The effect of his speech? Some mocked, some wanted to hear more, and some believed. This is the outcome one might expect from any faithful preaching of the Christian worldview.

So, we now want to ask, how do these two themes go together? (1) Non-Christian religions have deep insights into the truth, and (2) they are deficient at the point that makes the crucial difference. We get significant help to answer this from Romans 1:18-23. Paul tells his readers two things. First, that they know God. He doesn't say they know something about God, or that there is some force up there they are in touch with. He tells them they know God, with his eternal power and deity (Romans 1:20). Power and deity are the very essence of God's nature. But then, second, he says they have not processed this knowledge rightly. Indeed, he says they have suppressed the knowledge of God. The result? God let them become foolish.

There is a lot going on here. How can we know and ignore God at the same time? How can we see him so clearly we are without excuse, and at the same time exchange him (that is the word Paul uses) for something from the creation? We must make no mistake: this is an indictment of world religions, including individual expressions of faith. The speech in Acts addresses devout persons, including the Jews Paul met in a synagogue, as well as Greek philosophers he met in the marketplace. In Romans he is addressing all mankind, with a special focus on his own people, the Jews. The point is, no one escapes the accusing finger.

How different this view is from the typical beautiful coffee table book on the world's religions, where we are introduced to devout Tibetan monks on the mountains, to African tribal dancers with masks, as well as to Gothic churches in Europe. The impression given is of people all over the planet expressing their commitment to the holy or to something other, and that they do so in an atmosphere of beauty and tranquility. The New Testament tells a very different story. The bottom line is, it explains that people are running away from God and trying to escape their own accountability. God is revealing himself to them, and they do know him at some level, yet they deliberately twist their understanding so as to avoid the implications of their knowledge.

True Religion and False

BUT WHEN CHRIST HAD OFFERED FOR ALL TIME A SINGLE SACRIFICE FOR SINS, HE SAT DOWN AT THE RIGHT HAND OF GOD. (HEBREWS 10:12)

We are so used to looking at things from our earthly horizon upward, that it is hard to accept the biblical idea that it is God who reaches down. The popular idea of the religions is that they have their scriptures (the Quran, the Vedas, the Torah), their places of worship (temples, shrines, churches), and their wise teachers (Confucius, Muhammad, Jesus Christ). According to this idea, the teachers pretty much render the same message. We should love one another, give to the poor, have a disciplined life, etc. If we look around us, according to this view, we must conclude that our human probing after the truth falls into recognizable patterns.

According to the Bible, however, the fundamental issue we face is how to be right with God. What has separated us from him is neither our frailty nor our ignorance. It is our willful rebellion. When I first heard this diagnosis, I thought to myself, I am no rebel, nor would I wish to be separated from God. It did not occur to me that I was a sinner. That word was out of the movies or from a Puritan sermon for me. But the more I began really to know myself, the more I realized I was not so innocent. I could be unkind, proud, and ambitious. And whenever I had an opportunity really to know God I denied the experience or explained it away. I could be moved by great religious music or painters from the Dutch golden age. However, I was not willing to admit my life's goal was to be happy and safe, rather than to encounter God.

But God reached down to me. He came 'to seek and to save the lost' (Luke 19:10). The word 'lost' means without any meaningful relation to God and no real hope for the future. Some dear people explained the gospel to me and led me to faith. And I responded with my simple faith

The world religions have much to teach us. But this is only because God is making himself known to people, not because they are innocently probing upward, hoping to find some sort of guidance. When they do receive the knowledge of God they process it all wrong. Beginning with the knowledge of God they process it so that he emerges in a distorted way. Yet unless they somewhere had a sense of who God is, they could not be held responsible before him That leads to idolatry not true religion. But knowing this is actually liberating for us, because it clears the way to listen to what God is really saying. And thankfully God has not left us in our ignorance but has reached down, once for all, in his Son, to accomplish the redemption of his people. And today he continues to find them and to save them.

The Christian religion is true because God is God, and Jesus Christ is 'the way the truth and the life' (John 14:6). If there were any other way, however plausible, whereby we could be saved, God would have found it. If there were a less costly way than the death of his Son, surely, he would have found it.

But there is not. Thankfully, he was willing to pay the price to redeem us.

Discussion Questions:

1. What insights from some of the world's religions (outside of the Christian one) are right, or at least helpful?

2. Where do they fall short?

3. Does everyone have at least some decree of light? Enough to make them responsible?

4. Why does the Lord wait so long before finally establishing his truth?

Must I be Civil?

A LIE CAN TRAVEL HALF WAY AROUND THE WORLD WHILE THE TRUTH IS PUTTING ON ITS SHOES (CHARLES HADDON SPURGEON).

We face many trends today. Some of them present a serious threat to believing and proclaiming the Christian message. For that matter, some elements in the present atmosphere make it difficult to speak freely on certain issues at all. One of the most daunting challenges we encounter, at least in many Western countries, is the freedom to disagree. Sometimes the problem is that we're just not very good at it. But at other times, it is because we are in an atmosphere where disagreement is perceived as insulting. Here is a recent case in point. Fran Cowling, the

LGBT (lesbian, gay, bisexual, transgendered) Student Union representative at the University of Cardiff, said she would not appear on the stage of an important debate, unless Peter Tatchell was disinvited. His offense? Signing an open letter in the Observer promoting free speech and refusing to censor anyone who disagrees with various positions. In this case Tatchell defended the right to disagree with the claims of some transgendered people. Never mind that Tatchell is himself a well-known gay activist. Cowling judged that such a petition amounts to hatred of transgendered people. She went further and urged the university to cancel a lecture by Germaine Greer, a noted feminist who happens also to question the assertions about being transgendered. Greer sincerely doubts that surgery can change a man into a woman.[1] In her words, she argues that 'an unman is not necessarily a woman.'[2]

---

1. [https://www.theguardian.com/uk-news/2016/feb/13/peter-tatchell-snubbed-students-free-speech-veteran-gay-rights-activist]

2. [https://www.theguardian.com/education/2015/oct/23/petition-urges-cardiff-university-to-cancel-germain-greer-lecture]

Germaine Greer predictably objected to being gagged for her views. Now, note well that she is no friend of Christians, in that she openly criticizes the institution of marriage on many levels. She simply wants a hearing. In fairness, Fran Cowling is concerned that vulnerable people (such as the transgendered) not be further marginalized than they are. Christians ought to have some sympathies for such a view, since the Bible tells us to look out for the disenfranchised (Hebrews 1:27). But Cowling tags Tatchell and Greer's views 'transphobic.' Greer is puzzled and irritated, since she doesn't feel phobic toward anyone, but simply disagrees with some of the popular views out there. This argument at least deserves to be debated. This is another view with which we Christians ought to have much sympathy. Why should the right to debate a question be denied?

Whatever the merits of such cases, what is alarming is the atmosphere in which disagreement is considered hatred. Christians are not the only group accused of hate speech. If Christians are not the only targets of this kind of accusation, they certainly are in the crosshairs of a good many social pundits. No doubt it is easy to become over-sensitive and interpret everything as persecution. We're quite far from ancient Rome where it was illegal to be a Christian. Still, persecution is real enough. And the media do not report them with nearly the zeal they do when other minorities are mistreated. For example, we might consider the case of Nissa Hussain, who converted out of Islam to the Christian faith. He recently had to be moved to a safe house in Yorkshire because of so many attacks on him and his family. But almost no one knows about it. We need to ask why his case was hardly reported, when week after week hate crimes against non-Christian minorities are constantly in the headlines.

Teaching Christians How Not to Persuade

LET YOUR SPEECH ALWAYS BE GRACIOUS, SEASONED WITH SALT, SO THAT YOU MAY KNOW HOW YOU OUGHT TO ANSWER EACH PERSON (COLOSSIANS 4:6).

Preaching the gospel with success depends on the work of God's Holy Spirit. But we have been asked to use words, and to be persuasive.

We have been told to engage in Christian apologetics, the defense and commendation of the faith (1 Peter 3:15). Paul speaks of commending the gospel message by openly stating the truth of God's word to everyone's conscience (2 Corinthians 4:2). He is very concerned to do this with integrity, refusing manipulative speech (2 Corinthians 3:1; 5:12; 10:12; 1 Thessalonians 2:4-6). His audiences, whether accepting or not, recognized in him a capable persuader. King Agrippa's retort to Paul's long speech is revealing: 'In a short time would you persuade me to be a Christian?' (Acts 26:28). To which the apostle replied, 'Whether short or long, I would to God that not only you but also all who hear me this day might become such as I am – except for these chains' (he was at that point under arrest, Acts 26:29). The book you have in your hands is really a book of Christian apologetics.

There are obvious ways not to pursue when disagreeing with someone else. One is to become paranoid, and then angry and shrill. It is sometimes tempting to do this, since those who disagree with us seem to do it so unfairly. But we, of all people, ought to respect all people, even our 'enemies,' which the Bible requires us to love (Matthew 5:43-48).

Almost everyone has noticed the irony: the more we use social media the less we feel really comfortable really engaging with real persons. We often feel we have permission to say things over Facebook, Twitter, that we wouldn't dare say in person. Other unfair attacks might include assigning a negative label to them rather than evaluating their point of view in a reasonable manner. As an American I can well remember when to disagree with President Obama was considered racist (he was our first black President). I have been in conversations where to disagree with a woman has been called sexist. There certainly are racists and sexists in our societies who are not willing to look at issues because of their prejudice. But Christians ought to focus on the issues. Labeling someone rather than carefully examining their views is forbidden by Scripture. It is known technically as the *ad hominem* tactic, because instead of addressing the argument it addresses the man ('these people aren't like us'; 'you can't trust anyone from that part of the world'; 'what does he know, he's a liberal').

Honestly listening is difficult in a culture that rewards knee-jerk reactions to just about everything. But this is a good time to cultivate patience and confidence in the truth. One of my favorite Proverbs says, 'The one who states his case first seems right, until the other comes and examines him' (Proverbs 18:17). That doesn't mean the other person is always right, nor that we must somehow acquiesce to an opposite opinion. The chameleon may be admirable for its camouflage technique, but it is not an enviable human trait. Yet, empathetic listening is always a good move.

Another tactic, the opposite of lashing out at our enemies, is to withdraw. There are serious movements abroad telling Christians to get out of the public sphere and patiently bide the time until things become more tolerant. One such movement in North America is called the Benedict Option. The movement's leader, Rod Dreher, considers that the West is in such decline that there is little hope in trying to stave off the decay. Instead, we ought to retreat into monasteries such as the ones created by

Benedict of Nursia (c. A.D. 480-537). Benedict was sent to Rome by his parents, but what he saw there was so appalling that he fled to a forest in central Italy and began founding communities guided by his famous Rule, which is still practiced in monasteries today.

According to Dreher the purpose of this kind of retreat is not resignation but resistance, bringing with it the opportunity to build families and community as we wait for the world to improve. This view has a good deal of surface appeal. First, it appears to shield us from facing so many of the difficulties of a world that is falling apart at the seams. Second, it stresses community which is an attractive alternative to the alienation many people experience today. Third, it stresses discipline, virtue, character, qualities seemingly absent from the world outside.

However, there are serious problems with the withdrawal option. For starters it is too pessimistic about the world. Of course, there is terrible decadence, but there is also remarkable progress in areas such as health care, racial justice, women's rights and the like. As the Bible puts it, the wheat and the weeds are growing up together. The end of the world will indeed come, but it is not yet here. Second, this view puts the wrong kind of pressure on the church. While the community of believers can do many things, it cannot take the place of all legitimate institutions within God's creation. It cannot (and must not) seek to replace the state, or the family, or the school, though it certainly may articulate certain guiding principles for them. Third, and most important for our purposes, the Withdrawal view lacks compassion for the world. When we don't get our hands dirty and mix it up with unbelievers we lose the chance to engage in persuasion.

Being actively engaged in the world is not an option for Christians. Of course, we do it according to our stations, our talents, our calling. But just as the first century Christians were equipped by the apostolic preachers and writers to face what was an extremely difficult world, so may we have that same confidence today. Indeed, it has been observed that our advanced modern society resembles the Roman world of New Testament times more than the centuries between then and now.

A Few Guidelines

SO, BEING AFFECTIONATELY DESIROUS OF YOU, WE WERE READY TO SHARE WITH YOU NOT ONLY THE GOSPEL OF GOD BUT ALSO OUR OWN SELVES, BECAUSE YOU HAD BECOME VERY DEAR TO US (1 THESSALONIANS 2:8).

So then, how do we engage in the art of persuasion today? Here are some very needed guidelines, for what takes a lifetime to learn.

1. Know and believe the message. Describing his own work of persuasion, Paul makes a simple statement: 'Since we have the same spirit of faith according to what has been written, 'I believed, and so I spoke,' we also believe and so we speak' (2 Corinthians 4:13). He is quoting Psalm 116:10, a Scripture about standing firm in the midst of great trials.

   The gospel is summarized scores of times in the New Testament. At its center is what Paul tells the Corinthians: 'For I delivered to you as of first importance what I also received: that Christ died for our sins in accordance with the Scriptures, that he was buried, that he was raised on the third day in accordance with the Scriptures...'

(1 Corinthians 15:3-4). What should our response be to this message? To repent and believe and be baptized in the name of Jesus Christ (Acts 2:38). Simple, profound, and life-changing.

2. Discern, with God's help, where the message might find a point of contact with an unbeliever. We saw in the previous chapter what some of those places look like. There is a place in everyone, no matter how well hidden, where they know God unavoidably (Romans 1:19). Try to appeal to that awareness by highlighting it. It is often in a person's sense of right and wrong, though it can be other manifestations as well, such as the sense of beauty, a dissatisfaction with materialism, and so forth.

3. Discern, with God's help, where the place of resistance is. Everyone has a stumbling block, an idol which they hold on to doggedly, irrationally. Idols are often relatively good things made into absolutes. Money, sex, pride, family, music, these good gifts of the Lord's have

45

been made into objects of worship. We turn to the gift, forgetting the giver. When we find the individual's place of resistance this should allow us to find a place of impossibility within the unbelieving view. If all there is is money, how do you explain falling in love? If all there is is sex, how can you not turn another person into an object? If pride is always justified, how do you explain your failures? This kind of tactic may sound simple, but it really is not. People are complex; their aspirations as well as their flaws are often subtle.

4. Don't employ the uncivil manner we claim our opponents employ. We should refuse to demonize our unbelieving friends, as they sometimes do us. We want to spend as much time with them as possible. Ideally our non-Christian friend will say to us, 'We still don't agree, but you have represented my view fairly and sympathetically.' Show your friends that they are not some kind of project, but that you love them, whatever their

views.[3] But then also, don't be afraid to speak the powerful words of the gospel. They are God's power to change lives (Romans 1:16-17).

Discussion Questions:

1. Do you think it is getting harder to voice a dissenting opinion?

2. How does one balance listening with proclaiming?

3. What are some of the mistakes we can make when trying to persuade?

---

3. A good deal of this is common sense. Modern business practices have studied ways to disagree and yet still remain on the same team. See [https://www.fastcompany.com/3064577/the-right-way-and-right-reasons-to-disagree-with-your-boss].

Why Jesus Christ?

WHAT WAS OF DECISIVE IMPORTANCE WAS THAT GOD'S REVELATION IN JESUS CHRIST WAS OF AN ULTIMATE CHARACTER, DISCLOSING A NEW DIMENSION OF HUMAN EXISTENCE (GEORGES FLOROVSKY).

Whether we like it or not Jesus Christ won't go away. His name can even be heard as a curse word by people who don't have the slightest interest in him. Many people in the world agree that there is a God. But the idea that he has a Son who became a man and walked on the earth over two thousand years ago is far less popular. And yet there he is, and we must decide something about him.

Some people are simply embarrassed about Jesus. He has been called the 'scandal of particularity.' The scandal is that the great God of the universe could become so small, so petty, so particular, as to take on human qualities and live as a rabbi in the first century. It just doesn't seem worthy of the Almighty. Adding to the scandal is that Jesus told his disciples, 'I am the way and the truth and the life. No one comes to the Father except through me' (John 14:6). Such claims to exclusivity rub against the grain of today's people.

Instead of dismissing Jesus altogether, most people try to accommodate him to something like a wise person or a great teacher. One name for this view is Deism. Basically, Deism claims to be a natural religion, and to embrace all of the perceived advantages of the Christian faith without having to believe in miracles, divine inspiration of the Bible, and the like. Deists feel that various unique features of the Christian faith are an embarrassment because they are not shared with other religions. That there can be some kind of cosmic force is all right. But that God is also a particular Jewish man from first century Palestine, seems uncomfortable. That morality could be stated in generalities (do unto others as you would have them do unto you, be kind to the poor, and the like) is fine. But such strange sayings as, 'Leave the dead to bury their dead,' (Luke 9:60), or 'Whoever loves father and mother more than me is not worthy of me,' (Matthew 10:37) they find puzzling or even offensive.

Few have ever been as vehemently opposed to the Christian faith as Bertrand Russell (1872-1970). But he may well have represented what many would not have said in public, but nonetheless believed. In his notorious lecture, followed by a publication, titled 'Why I Am Not a Christian,' he levels several blows against the Christian faith.[1] To his credit, he recognizes that a Christian is not simply a person trying to live a moral life. One must have certain beliefs and must have a view that somehow Jesus is unique if they want legitimately to be called a Christian. I can well remember when I first became a believer my mother and father saying, 'of course we're Christians if we're not Jewish!' It's not enough just to strive to be a good person and appreciate Christian civilization.

---

1. Bertrand Russell, 'Why I Am Not a Christian,' presented in 1927 before the National Secular Society, New York: Simon & Schuster, 1957.

Russell then goes on to attack much about the Christian faith, including the integrity of Jesus Christ. This is quite rare and it's almost refreshing. Most people will try to hold Jesus in high regard, but without crediting him with being divine. Russell rather condescendingly tells his audience that Jesus was unrealistic, and that most professing Christians do not practice what Jesus taught. For example, they do not turn the other cheek, nor refuse to judge others. He also faults Jesus for seeming to teach that his second advent was quite imminent, whereas in fact we are still waiting. And, predictably, he objects to Jesus' teaching on eternal punishment, which he finds to be cruel.

It is surprising that someone of Russell's brilliance could be so naïve about the way Jesus' teaching works. This world-class philosopher and mathematician was quite deficient in understanding the Bible, unless he was being insincere. Every child in Sunday School should know that turning the other cheek and refusing to judge are, in contrast to the Pharisees' attitudes of superiority, and not statements about politics. Jesus' statements about the nearness of the kingdom of God require some deeper thought. For example, Jesus said, 'There are some standing here who will not taste death until they see the Son of Man coming in his kingdom' (Matthew 16:28). If he meant the second coming or the end of history, then clearly it did not happen in the lifetime of his listeners. But if he meant the central manifestation of his kingdom, the resurrection, then many did live to see it.

More disturbing are the charges about eternal punishment. Indeed, these are among the most difficult teachings for contemporary people to hear. We don't want to believe in a God who would send people to hell. Russell suggests Jesus got perverse pleasure out of describing the pains of hell. These are serious charges that deserve an answer. The basic answer is that God is just and will not leave guilt unpunished. If we think about this would we want any other kind of universe? Would we want a Hitler or a Stalin to get away with their crimes? We would not. But, somehow, we don't imagine our own 'crimes' are anything like those of these two monsters. At one level they aren't. But at another level, any transgression against God, however small in our eyes, is fraught with heavy implications. To offend God is not simply to cross a couple of minor lines. It is, as one person put it, cosmic treason. Do we seriously want a world without consequences for immoral behavior?

The good news is that as serious as our transgressions are, God's love is even more serious. The Christian view is that God exists in three Persons: Father, Son and Holy Spirit. The view also understands that the Second Person became a man and endured so much on behalf of his people. He was sent into the world not to condemn it but that the world could be saved through him (John 3:17). It is quite misguided to suggest there is any kind of pleasure in the death of a sinner, quite the opposite (Ezekiel 33:11). But the idea that we are sinners, and that we cannot rescue ourselves is quite repugnant to Bertrand Russell, who states in this essay and elsewhere, that he does not wish to live in the world the churches have made, but in one where all we need is human effort. He must have closed his eyes to the atrocities of

World War I, the dreadful outcome of human effort.

To his credit, again, Russell refuses the typical caricature about Christ being a good moral teacher. Jesus did not claim to be a good moral guide but to be God himself come down from heaven, expecting his followers to worship him. When Jesus made his stupendous assertion, 'Before Abraham was, I am,' (John 8:58) the religious leaders picked up stones to kill him. Why? Because Jesus was claiming to be the God who revealed himself to Moses in the Old Testament. He declared to Moses, 'I am that I am' which in Hebrew is a statement using the verb to be, meaning that God is, and there is no other! The religious leaders knew what he was saying, though they hated it. C.S. Lewis put it this way: 'Either this man was, and is, the Son of God, or else a madman or something worse. You can shut him up for a fool, you can spit at him and kill him as a demon or you can fall at his feet and call him Lord and God, but let us not come with any patronizing nonsense about being a great human teacher. He has not left that open to us. He did not intend to.'[2]

Why Did Jesus Come to Us?

I AM THE WAY, AND THE TRUTH, AND THE LIFE. NO ONE COMES TO THE FATHER EXCEPT THROUGH ME (JOHN 14:6).

It's not that Jesus did not teach marvelous moral precepts. A casual read through the Sermon on the Mount will reveal otherwise. It's that his moral teachings were not meant to be a way of self-improvement or merely a path to noble behavior. They are meant to be the fruit of a life surrendered to him for redemption. And this redemption can only be accomplished when a believer comes to Jesus for the forgiveness of sins. Jesus Christ, the Second Person of the Holy Trinity became human in order that he could obey God perfectly and then receive on himself the full consequences of God's anger against our guilt. His resurrection from the dead is the proof that such a transaction has occurred in history. That is why Paul ended his message to

---

2. C. S. Lewis, *Mere Christianity*, New York: HarperCollins, 2001, p. 53.

the Athenians with Christ's resurrection, and the appeal to repent. (See Acts 17:22-34)

No other religion, no other philosophy, however popular, has anything remotely resembling this view. As one person has put it, the Christian faith is the only religion whose God has wounds. All the others propose a path for human improvement. The Christian faith proposes a path for human forgiveness and for being right with God. To put it quite negatively, if various religions were a legitimate path to the truth, why then did Christ have to suffer so very much? His painful death on the Roman gallows was not an example, but the atonement for all evil. It was the only way to pay for our transgressions. Here is how one sage put it: 'The cross of Jesus clearly indicates that there was no less costly method to wipe out our sin before the holy God.'[3] As one popular evangelist put it: in the world religions the message is, 'do, do, do'. In the Christian faith the message is, 'done!'

---

3. Werner Gitt, *Questions I Have Always Wanted to Ask*, Neptune, NJ: Loiseaux, 1992, p. 89.

There is no more eloquent expression of who Jesus is, and what he came to do, than in the opening words of the Gospel of John:

> IN THE BEGINNING WAS THE WORD, AND THE WORD WAS WITH GOD, AND THE WORD WAS GOD. HE WAS IN THE BEGINNING WITH GOD. ALL THINGS WERE MADE THROUGH HIM, AND WITHOUT HIM WAS NOT ANYTHING MADE THAT WAS MADE. IN HIM WAS LIFE, AND THE LIFE WAS THE LIGHT OF MEN. THE LIGHT SHINES IN THE DARKNESS, AND THE DARKNESS HAS NOT OVERCOME IT (JOHN 1:1-5).

Jesus is likened to the divine Word because he reveals the truth and he is the truth. The term translated Word is *logos* which here means divine self-expression. Notice not only was the Word with God but the Word was God. We have here a clear statement of what Christians have believed down through the ages. God is one God, but in three Persons (only the first two are mentioned here, although the third, the Holy Spirit, is cited soon thereafter, in John 1:32-33). The Second Person was in the beginning, thus eternal. And he had a hand in the creation of the world. But he also came into this world, to shine on it his invincible light.

Had not the Second Person come into our world, to reveal all truth, we would be lost. We would be in darkness. Furthermore, we would still be wallowing in our sins. For Jesus Christ humbled himself and became obedient to the point of death on a cross, in order that we may not have to endure the eternal punishment Bertrand Russell so ridiculed (Philippians 2:8; Hebrews 2:17).

Discussion Questions:

1.   Why do you think some people are more or less comfortable believing in God, but most uncomfortable with Jesus Christ?

2.   Where did Bertrand Russell misrepresent Jesus Christ?

3.   What was the main purpose for Jesus' coming to earth?

4.   Why does the Gospel of John liken Christ to the Word?

What Kind of Book is the Bible?

THE HOLY SCRIPTURES ARE OUR LETTERS FROM HOME. (ST. AUGUSTINE)

The Bible is by far the best-selling book in the world. Some five billion copies have been printed and distributed. This compares to one of the next best-sellers, Chairman Mao's Red Book, which has sold about 800 million. Harry Potter has sold 400 million. The entire Bible has been translated into 349 languages and counting. Some 2,123 languages have at least one book of the Bible in that language. These facts in themselves do not tell us what we should believe about the Bible. But they suggest it has had, and continues to have, an astonishing impact.

Why would this be? There are all kinds of claims about what kind of book the Bible is. One commonly held answer is that it is a library. The Bible contains many different books which are written in different literary genres by different authors from different times. These books represent the experiences people had of God or and his actions toward them at a particular time. They were combined quite late and bound between two covers. David Lose, writing in the Huffington Post, says that for some people, the Bible is 'Not unlike a family scrapbook that's been passed down through the generations, [wherein] the various bits and pieces combine to tell a story about this particular family of faith and the God they worship. In this way, the Bible invites readers to enter into the narrative truth it provides and make this story their own.'[1]

According to the Bible itself, its pages are not human reflections but a revelation from God, which contain both truth and power. 2 Timothy 3:15-16 tells us the sacred writings are able to make us 'wise for salvation through faith in Jesus Christ' (3:15). To be wise for salvation means we have all

1. David Lose, 'What Kind of Book Is the Bible?', *The Huffington Post* [http://www huffingtonpost.com/david-lose/bible-what-kind-of-book_b_846579.html].

we need in order to be relocated from darkness to light, from being eternally lost to being redeemed as one of God's children. The text goes on to explain, 'All Scripture is breathed out by God and profitable for teaching, for reproof, for correction, and for training in righteousness, that the man of God may be competent, equipped for every good work' (2 Timothy 3:16-17). This is an astonishing assertion about a collection of books.

A Covenant Book

AND THE LORD SPOKE ALL THESE WORDS SAYING, I AM THE LORD YOUR GOD, WHO BROUGHT YOU OUT OF THE LAND OF EGYPT, OUT OF THE HOUSE OF SLAVERY. YOU SHALL HAVE NO OTHER GODS BEFORE ME (EXODUS 20:1-3).

The Bible indeed has many parts, but they all converge to give us something like a constitutional document. When the people of Israel arrived at Mount Sinai and received the ten commandments, something much more than a particular people receiving the divine law was at stake. The entire event was rather terrifying, which signaled its significance. The people were told to stay away from the mountain and to be hallowed, that is, specially dedicated to God. The trumpet would be very loud and the mountain full of smoke and fire (Exodus 19:9-25).

Moses ascended the mountain and was given the two tablets of the law to be a possession for God's people. They were to keep them, along with Moses' other writings, beside the great ark of the covenant (Deuteronomy 31:24-29). They were to be a witness of the people's identity (Hebrews 9:4). Thus, the two tablets, combined with Moses' other writings, were far more than a set of laws, or than even a history of the people's encounters with God. The subsequent Scriptures, including the New Testament documents, are but extensions of these foundational papers. Thus, the apostle Peter quite naturally associates Paul's writing with 'the other Scriptures' (2 Peter 3:16). The Book of Hebrews tells us we, God's people, have come to the true Mount Zion, and we are welcome there along with the entire church. But it warns, 'See that you do not refuse him who is speaking' (Hebrews 12:25). Where does he speak? The Bible!

Recognizing the great diversity of the different styles and genres of biblical literature should not lessen the unity of the sixty-six books. Quite the contrary. It is one of the Bible's great originalities that it contains history, law, wisdom, songs, prophecy and much more, all converging to compose the same basic message. What is that message?

It is this, spoken by John the Baptist: 'The time is fulfilled, and the kingdom of God is at hand; repent and believe in the gospel' (Mark 1:15). The kingdom of God is a realm. Specifically it is the realm where God is ruling and spreading his righteousness. The kingdom was announced from ancient times but is now initiated with the appearance of Jesus Christ. Although we still await the final manifestation of God's kingdom, the inauguration has occurred in the death and resurrection of Jesus Christ. The Bible, from beginning to end, attests to this kingdom, and to the access we have in the gospel, the good news that God so loves us that he gave his only Son so that whoever believes in him would have eternal life (John 3:16).

The first five books of the Bible are known as the Pentateuch. They recount the history of creation, the fall of man, and the early gathering by God of a people for himself. The subsequent books take us into the time when God's people were captives, released and finally received a land of their own. We are introduced to the people's prayer book, the Psalms, and their books of wisdom, Job, the Proverbs, Ecclesiastes and the Songs of Solomon. Then Israel's unfaithfulness is described. Despite the constant admonitions of the prophets, God's people had to dwell in occupied territory because of their treachery. But God did not forget his people. At the right time, he sent his Son, Jesus Christ, to dwell on earth, to teach, to perform miracles, and then to die and be raised up for our salvation. His story is recorded in the four Gospels. The book of Acts tells of the beginnings of the church. And then we have the letters to God's people, Paul's, James', Peter's, the author of Hebrews, and John's. The very last book of the Bible describes the final unfolding of history before heaven and hell.

The Bible records the successive unfolding of God's revelation. What is present in seed form in the Old Testament becomes full-grown in the New. As one popular saying goes, the New is in the Old concealed, the Old is in the New revealed.[2] Genesis 3:15 tells us the seed of the woman would crush the head of the seed of the serpent, whereas the seed of the serpent would bruise the head of the seed of the woman. This rather veiled form of the promise of Christ's death and resurrection becomes crystal clear in the New Testament. As the apostle Paul says, 'For all the promises of God find their yes in him' (2 Corinthians 1:20).

---

2. Possibly first spoken by Augustine.

Any Errors?

SANCTIFY THEM IN THE TRUTH; YOUR WORD IS TRUTH. (JOHN 17:17)

The Bible is God's self-disclosure. Unlike other so-called sacred texts, the Bible is also fully human. Each author has a personality and shows preferences for different images and the selection of themes. There are four Gospels, and each conveys the orientation of its author. Paul's letters are different from James'. 1 and 2 Kings have slightly different emphases from 1 and 2 Chronicles, even though they are writing about the same events and persons. This diversity is actually a great strength.

There are those who would like to see this diversity as carrying errors. I remember as a fairly new Christian sitting at a table with a seasoned liberal theologian. He was rather making fun of what he thought was my naïve fundamentalism. He asked whether I believed there were any errors in the Bible. I said something like, 'God would not be making mistakes.' But he pressed me. So, I finally asked him for an example. He said that in one place Jesus tells the disciples 'whoever is not with me is against me' (Matthew 12:30), but in another he says, 'for the one who is not against us is for us' (Mark 9:40).

At first, I thought, what do I do with this? But it did not take me long to see that the two passages were talking about entirely different things. In the first instance the Pharisees were accusing Jesus of casting out demons by the prince of demons. Instead, he explained, he was busy destroying the works of Satan and using the power of the Holy Spirit to cast out demons. Anyone who does not believe in the Holy Spirit is against Jesus Christ. In the second case he is teaching that one does not always have to use the name of Christ to be working on the same side as he. The first addresses hostile people, the second addresses allies. They both say, in different ways, that neutrality is not possible.

To be sure, not every apparent contradiction is quite so easy to resolve. Because this is God's Word, none of us will be able to unravel every mystery. But we don't need to in order to understand the basic message of the Bible. One of the teachings the Reformers gave us was the perspicuity of Scripture. That's a fancy word meaning clarity. To be sure, there are difficulties. Some texts are harder to understand than others (2 Peter 3:16 says parts of Paul are hard to understand!).

If we are worried about this, we can rest assured that the same God who gave us his Word has made available the power to understand it. 'So shall my word be that goes out from my mouth; it shall not return to me empty, but it shall accomplish that which I purpose,' Isaiah tells us (Isaiah 55:11). It can do that because it is 'more powerful than a two-edged sword' (See Hebrews 4:12). The Lord wants us to know the gospel. That is because he wants us to know his own self. 'You have said, 'Seek my face.' My heart says to you, 'Your face, LORD, do I seek.'' (Psalm 27:8). How can we do that? Who can see God? 'The pure in heart' (Matthew 5:8). But how can we become pure? By trusting the gospel, the good news, the Word of the Lord, which will lead us to meet the Lord of the Word.

Discussion Questions:

1. What is meant by the term 'covenant'? Why do we call the Bible a covenant book?

2. What is meant by the 'Kingdom of God'?

3. What do we mean by calling God's revelation progressive?

4. If we think we see a problem or a contradiction in Scripture what should be our attitude?

Why is there Cruelty?

THE ULTIMATE TRAGEDY IS NOT THE OPPRESSION AND CRUELTY BY THE BAD PEOPLE BUT THE SILENCE OVER THAT BY THE GOOD PEOPLE (MARTIN LUTHER KING, JR).

I was attending a conference. One night, the presenters were from IJM (International Justice Mission). The group specializes in stopping sex trafficking around the world. That night they showed a brief documentary with footage of little girls in their nightshirts being sold off to predators in an obscure village somewhere in the Southern hemisphere. I had to leave the room, go up to my hotel chamber, where I vomited much of the night.

What I had seen was evil, in the raw. The poor children were sold off to wealthy marauders to use as their toys and abuse them at will. How could anyone even think about taking a child at the beginning of their life and exploit them to satisfy their lusts? My nausea soon turned into rage, and for a brief moment I thought about going over to this place and gunning down the brigands. Of course, I realized this would have been futile, and that the IJM was doing the best possible job of ferreting out not only the predators, but the parents, and the greater group that could allow such debauchery. Indeed, as was explained, this corruption was systemic, requiring resistance at various levels if there was any hope of reversal.

I had been a Christian for a number of years when I had this experience. So, I knew the Bible's teaching: 'For all have sinned and fallen short of the glory of God' (Romans 3:23). And I believed it. But that statement seemed rather abstract, compared with the brutal reality of ruining a little child's life for the sake of lust. I had so much to learn.

The Bible is in fact brutally honest about the human condition. The same Book of Romans from which this statement is taken describes all of humanity as 'under the power of sin,' which, it explains, means:

'NONE IS RIGHTEOUS, NO, NOT ONE; NO ONE UNDERSTANDS; NO ONE SEEKS FOR GOD. ALL HAVE TURNED ASIDE; TOGETHER THEY HAVE BECOME WORTHLESS; NO ONE DOES GOOD, NOT EVEN ONE.'
'THEIR THROAT IS AN OPEN GRAVE; THEY USE THEIR TONGUES TO

DECEIVE.' 'THE VENOM OF ASPS IS UNDER THEIR LIPS.' 'THEIR MOUTH IS FULL OF CURSES AND BITTERNESS.' 'THEIR FEET ARE SWIFT TO SHED BLOOD; IN THEIR PATHS ARE RUIN AND MISERY, AND THE WAY OF PEACE THEY HAVE NOT KNOWN.' 'THERE IS NO FEAR OF GOD BEFORE THEIR EYES' (3:10-18).

On nearly every page of the Bible, mankind is described as so corrupt it grieved the Lord, their Creator, who regretted that he had made them in the first place (Genesis 6:5-6). There are chapters in the Book of Judges that are virtually unreadable, so ruthless is their description of the cruelty of people against people.

So why was I so repulsed? And why am I often repulsed when hearing of human cruelty? This reveals another trait in human beings besides our cruelty. We have a conscience. We not only know that some things are wrong, but we can be deeply distressed by them. Does everyone have a conscience? Even the predators in the village? To be sure, they have gone so far down the path of corruption we may wonder if they have any moral sense left at all. The New Testament describes some people as having a 'seared conscience,' that is, a moral sense so deeply scarred there is not much left of it. The most pessimistic thinker, the darkest philosophy, have nothing over the dark words of Scripture about the human condition.

And yet, even the most cruel people have pockets where they are still aware of right and wrong. It has been demonstrated, for example, that even these horrible predators who will sell little girls into slavery would not subject their own daughters to abuse. The abortion doctor also works hard to save the lives of children already born. The Mafia boss goes to church. These contradictions testify to the vestiges of goodness in the world. There is beauty, justice, generosity. How can these coexist with evil?

This contradiction tells us something crucially important about our natures. As a matter of fact we would not even be sensitive to the presence of evil, were we not made moral beings. Even though desperately fallen, we remain God's image-bearers (Genesis 1:26-27; James 3:9; Psalm 8:6-8). How can we be both inclined to evil and morally aware, even capable of considerable good? Strange but true, all of us are living contradictions.

Why the Wait?

I WILL BEAR THE INDIGNATION OF THE LORD BECAUSE I HAVE SINNED AGAINST HIM, UNTIL HE PLEADS MY CAUSE AND EXECUTES JUDGMENT FOR ME. (MICAH 7:9)

If God is sorry he made us, then why did he bother? We may not be able to answer that question, at least in the way it is posed. Instead, we may assert two fundamental truths. The first is that God is against evil. That sounds abstract. God is revolted against evil, he hates it, he weeps over it. The powerful Old Testament prophet Habakkuk looks at the armies of God's enemies, the Chaldeans, coming to devastate the people of Israel, and he is forced to ask, 'Are you not from everlasting, O Lord my God, my Holy One?... You who are of purer eyes than to see evil and cannot look at wrong, why do you idly look at traitors and are silent when the wicked swallows up the man more righteous than he?' (Habakkuk 1:12-13) There is an honest question. But it's based on the certainty that God does not tolerate evil. In this story Habakkuk is told to wait and see.

What should he wait for? Ultimately, God will judge the earth. Really? Yes, because he is God, and no universe can stand without facing the highest court of all, the bench where God sits and judges. So, why does he not get on with it? That is a lesson I have been trying to learn during my entire life. I've made some progress, but I am not there yet. God's timing is not my timing. I am in good company. Many times the Psalmists and the prophets ask, 'How long, O Lord?' One of my favorite negro Spirituals begins this way, 'God don't come when you want him to, but he's always right on time.' Just how long can this world last in its present condition? We are not exactly told, except that Jesus declares that there will be wars and rumors of wars, there will be persecutions, and there will also be the spreading of the good news of the gospel before the end (see Luke 21).

And that is the second fundamental truth. Although God by rights could simply condemn and destroy the world, he has chosen to show his mercy on his people and delay the end until they have been able to meet him and become reconciled to him. This takes time. It means missionaries and evangelists and justice-workers like IJM must penetrate deeply into alien cultures, showing people from every kind of background how God has loved them, even while they were yet sinners, to bring them new life (Romans 5:8-11).

Who is to Blame?

And you were dead in the trespasses and sins in which you once walked, following the course of this world ... (Ephesians 2:1-2).

Here comes a hard question. Because the answer is an apparent contradiction. Not a real one, mind you. On the one hand there is no way around it: we, human beings, are at fault. That is another lesson I am still learning. My heart is crooked. Most people who know me think I am a good guy, a lovely person. But the truth is, given the opportunity, I am capable of some pretty bad things. One of my friends puts it this way: if you were sure no one were looking, even God, would you … (fill-in the blank). I don't think I could ever abuse a small child. But, given the right circumstances, and with no restraints, I believe I could do the equivalent in cruelty, just to gain advantage. Now, before you stop reading because you are repulsed let me reassure you that God is busy at work in all of us, restraining us from doing our worst. And we still exhibit the traits of his image-bearers.

Are there no mitigating circumstances? Certainly. Upbringing plays a part. So does the culture in which we are born. To the more privileged among us, we have a greater responsibility to be generous and help others. The child of a drug addict has less of a chance than the child of righteous parents. But still, the hard truth, the one I am still trying to learn, is that there is an inclination or a propensity for wrongdoing in each of us.

On the other hand, the second truth is that God is utterly in control of everything that comes to pass. This is the second truth, which appears contradictory to the first. Is it human beings? Or is it God? The answer is both, but not in the same way. God ordains everything that comes to pass. If we diminish this truth, then we diminish God. A God who is less than omnipotent is simply not God. God ordains everything that comes to pass. But the way he does it utilizes what we may call secondary causes. For example, he causes crops to grow, but he uses rain. When the secondary causes are circumvented we call that a miracle, a rare and special intervention.

He is somehow the cause of evil, but, yet, not accountable for it. The Westminster Confession of Faith puts it this way:

> GOD FROM ALL ETERNITY, DID, BY THE MOST WISE AND HOLY COUNSEL OF HIS OWN WILL, FREELY, AND UNCHANGEABLY ORDAIN WHATSOEVER COMES TO PASS; YET SO, AS THEREBY NEITHER IS GOD THE AUTHOR OF SIN, NOR IS VIOLENCE OFFERED TO THE WILL OF THE CREATURES; NOR IS THE LIBERTY OR CONTINGENCY OF SECOND CAUSES TAKEN AWAY, BUT RATHER ESTABLISHED.

This is a remarkably balanced statement. It would be hard to find words putting God's sovereignty more powerfully: from all eternity, by his own will, unchangeably ordain ... And then, without any embarrassment, it goes on to say he is not the author of sin. What can this mean? An author is the responsible agent. The Book of James tells us that when we are tempted, we mustn't say, I am tempted of God, for he cannot tempt anyone (James 1:13). So, somehow, God has made the world and us human beings in such a way that when we sin it is not he making us do it. Indeed, when we do anything, it is not because God pushes a button.

The language of the Confession is important: neither does God violate our wills, nor our freedom, but he establishes secondary causes. What does this mean? When crops grow it has rained and the sun has shone. These are secondary causes, that is, God does not ordinarily make things grow by miracle or direct intervention. To put it negatively, when we engage in wrongdoing we cannot say it is because God makes us do it. He may have ordained it from all eternity, so that ultimately there is a final cause in his decrees. But he has made the world so real that it is responsible for its behavior.

If your head is spinning as you read this, you are in good company! Because we are finite creatures we are not equipped to understand this. But we can still believe it. And we can live with it. The most extraordinary day after Christ's resurrection is the day of Pentecost. This is the day when the Holy Spirit was poured out on the multitudes, leading them to speak in different languages. When Peter describes the events that led to Pentecost, he says, 'This Jesus, delivered up according to the definite plan and foreknowledge of God, you crucified and killed by the hands of lawless men' (Acts 2:23). His declaration of God's plan does not remove from the guilt of the perpetrators. They knew it, and many of them repented.

Go Ahead and Do Something

AS I LIVE, DECLARES THE LORD GOD, I HAVE NO PLEASURE IN THE DEATH OF THE WICKED, BUT THAT THE WICKED TURN FROM HIS WAYS AND LIVE (EZEKIEL 33:11).

Our theological conundrum should not lead us to a life of speculation, but to a life of sorrow for our sin, and then one of helping others to overcome evil. We each have different callings so that there is not a one-size-fits-all remedy for the world's evils. But there is always something we can do, according to our gifts and calling.

As I often like to put it, we have moved from being faced with the problem of evil, to the problem of good. How can it be, in such a world gone wrong, that God loves us and is doing so much for us? That one has even less of an easy answer than the issue of God's power and our responsibility. How can God love us? The best we can do is simply to revel in his love and not try to find a motive for it.

Discussion Questions:

1. Why is there evil in the world? Can every instance of suffering be traced to a particular act of disobedience?

2. How can it be fair that everyone without exception is a sinner?

3. Why does God not put an end to injustice now, rather than at an appointed time later?

4. How may we be sure that God, though sovereign, is not the author of sin?

5. How is Jesus Christ the comprehensive remedy for sin and evil?

Is Sex a Problem?

INSTEAD OF IGNORING OUR DIFFERENCES, WE NEED TO ACCEPT AND TRANSCEND THEM (SHERYL SANDBERG).

Why should we bring up the subject of sex in a book on apologetics? Several reasons. First, our gender is clearly an important part of our identity. One of the characteristics of the teenage years is coming to grips with the sexual impulse. It is one of God's loveliest gifts. Too often Christians have advocated pure abstinence, thinking that abstinent behavior is somehow closer to godliness than the messy business of sex. Most of us are meant to enjoy this gift, albeit within the confines of marriage.

Second, while to be sure sexuality can be overblown, it has become an important issue as modern culture struggles to deal with departures from traditional marriage. Recently a friend of mine visited a church while on holiday. The liturgy was solid, even beautiful. But when it came to the Bible text for the day, something strange occurred. The minister read Genesis 1:24-27. When he came to verse 27, he simply read these words: 'So God created man in his own image, in the image of God he created them.' But if you look up this verse it has a third phrase: 'male and female he created them.' But that was simply left out. Presumably the reader wanted to avoid a sensitive subject. Perhaps he wanted not to offend gay people, or transgendered people. But the text from Genesis asserts a crucial truth about the way God has made the world. Nothing to be embarrassed about. We mustn't just tiptoe away.

Unfortunately, though, this area has become a battlefield. In many of our countries we speak of the LGBT community. These initials stand for lesbian, gay, bisexual and transgendered people. Recently some have added the initial Q, which stands for queer. This used to be a slur, but it is now seen as a positive, if ironic, defense of objectors to 'heteronormativity,' that is to anyone believing that being male and female should be the norm. It might be a stretch to call the LGBTQ people a community, since it is not tightly organized, nor does everyone belonging to it feel a strong kinship with everyone else in it. Yet, there are centers in various towns and groups in many universities composed of people of such leanings. Increasingly, to favor traditional marriage is to be on the defensive.

Third, many of those advocating the rights of LGBTQ people have an agenda, one which is not friendly to the Christian position. There are days of gay pride, and campaigns against phobic people, pleas to populate films with more gays or transgendered folks, etc. Remember the case of Fran Cowling at the University of Cardiff who fought against what she saw as the victimization of transgendered people. There is even an LGBTQ Month, and a national 'coming out day'. What is striking about all this is the sense that history is moving in a direction of tolerance, and those that oppose it are really in the way and do not belong. Recently the former American Vice-President belittled a defender of traditional marriage and declared that the American people had evolved toward the acceptance of alternative sexualities. The law is on his side, increasingly approving of gay marriage and other lifestyles. In my own family, there are gay people who feel they have lived too long 'in the closet' and now are finally free to marry other people.

Defensive or Affirmative?

AND SUCH WERE SOME OF YOU. BUT YOU WERE WASHED, YOU WERE SANCTIFIED, YOU WERE JUSTIFIED IN THE NAME OF THE LORD JESUS CHRIST AND BY THE SPIRIT OF OUR GOD (1 CORINTHIANS 6:11).

What should Christians who believe the Bible do in the face of such an admittedly compelling narrative? There are of course clear biblical texts forbidding same-sex relations and the confusion of genders. Leviticus 18:22 and 20:13 clearly condemn having sexual relations with a person of the same sex. Romans 1:26-27 and 1 Corinthians 6:9 do the same in the New Testament. Such verses have great authority, as do any clear ordinances from Scripture. But in doing Christian apologetics we want to persuade people with more than negative commandments. Years ago, there was an anti-drug campaign with the slogan: 'Just say no'. Needless to say it was not very effective. We need something to say yes to, as we renounce bad practices.

There are a number of helpful arguments along the way. One of them is to show according to recent polls how few avowed gay people there are compared to the rest of the population. The figure in the United States is 3.4 per cent. There may be many secret gays and the statistics vary according to geographic location. But from the rhetoric, such as the Vice-President saying the American people have evolved, we might get the impression that the vast population of Americans are gay. Similarly, for the transgendered, 0.3 per cent of the American population identify this way. And yet issues such as the use of bathrooms and joining the military are constantly in the news. The argument from percentages are not conclusive, since we are dealing with a moral issue. Yet it is significant that the advocates are so much louder than their numbers suggest.

Another helpful argument along the way is the testimony of people who have been involved in the gay lifestyle but have changed their minds. One of the most compelling is by Rosaria Champaign Butterfield, The Secret Thoughts of an Unlikely Convert.[1] She recounts how she moved from being a driving force in the Lesbian community of her university to becoming an advocate of traditional marriage. Another moving account is by Sam Allberry, a pastor from Maidenhead, UK, who himself struggles with same-sex attraction, but has found peace within the confines of chastity.[2] Ministries to the sexually broken, such as Harvest, will tell you that many, if not most LGBTQ people are not settled in their positions. Indeed, many of them are profoundly unhappy and guilt-ridden.[3]

---

1. Pittsburgh, PA: *Crown and Covenant*, 2012.

2. Sam Allberry, *Is God Anti-Gay?* Epsom, Surrey: The Good Book Company, 2013.

3. See the resources of Harvest Ministries [http://www.harvestusa.org/].

Back to Genesis

SO GOD CREATED MAN IN HIS OWN IMAGE, IN THE IMAGE OF
GOD HE CREATED HIM; MALE AND FEMALE HE CREATED THEM.
(GENESIS 1:27)

However, the most fundamental argument for traditional marriage is from the original configuration of creation. When we look at the way God created the man and the woman we can't help but be swept up in the romance of it all. Interestingly, marriage is presented in Genesis 2 as God's solution for human loneliness (2:18). After his death-like anesthesia, a portent to the self-sacrifice needed for true love, Adam awoke to behold his gorgeous partner. He was delighted and proceeded to sing the first love song (2:23). To be sure, procreation and populating the earth are a part of the larger picture of marriage (1:28). The family, then, is a fundamental unit for human society. But there is far more to marriage than sexual union and offspring. There is the beauty of the ultimate friendship between one man and one woman. The Song of Solomon gives an idea about the loveliness of the special attraction between a man and a woman. And, in this fallen world, which is yet being redeemed, marriage symbolizes the union between Christ and his church (Ephesians 5:32). Just as a man pursues his mate, taking vows, holding her tight, providing for her and sacrificing for her, so

Jesus pursues the lost, embraces them and brings them to heaven, all because of his sacrifice at Calvary.[4]

Very little of this can be reproduced in a gay relationship. Certainly, there can be love, sacrifice, and friendship. But it is the very difference between the two genders – male and female, each made after the image of God, yet each in their distinctive way – that makes for the high complement of opposites: a place where truly the whole is greater than the sum of the parts. Surely one of the reasons that gay unions are called 'dishonorable' in Scripture is because there is no honor in reaching out to someone who is like oneself. Jesus often remarked that 'if you love those that love you what reward do you have?' (Matthew 5:46).

Does this sound harsh? It is meant to sound beautiful. There is something lovely about 'the way of a man with a maid' (Proverbs 30:19 KJV). It needs to be said that gender relations are hardly limited to marriage. Men and women relate in all kinds of different ways in society, from simple friendships at work and school, and so much more. For that matter, so do men with men and women with women. One of the negative effects of the crusade for same-sex relations today is that, ironically,

4. One of the most helpful books on this entire subject is by David Powlison, *Making All Things New: Restpring Joy to the Sexually Broken*, Wheaton, IL: Crossway, 2017.

true non-sexual same-sex friendships are denigrated. Some readers are embarrassed to discover that David and Jonathan had a passionate companionship in the Old Testament times (see 1 Samuel 18:3). But such attachments are very real, though they have nothing to do with sexual relations.

Civil Rights

If the Bible speaks against same-sex sexual relations, it also strongly advocates civil rights for every person. This is because each human being is God's image-bearer. We need to be reminded of this, because disagreement with someone's lifestyle should not mean depriving them of their civil rights. When I was a lad, many of my friends and I simply tarred gay people as weird or perverted. We had no idea how to handle a young person who was really struggling with his or her sexual identity. As an adult I am trying to learn to treat gay or transgendered people as fully human, I now believe their sexual orientation should not be a reason to keep them from their full rights. If we are worried about predators , then we should not think that is a deviation uniquely connected to being gay or transgendered. There are plenty of predators in the heterosexual group as well.

What about church membership? I believe the right view is, if a gay-inclined person is willing to keep his or her leanings in check, there should be no problem being a member in good standing in the church. As a matter of fact, the same thing goes for a heterosexual. Just because that person is attracted to the opposite sex does not give them the right to wander into illicit relationships outside the bonds of marriage.

This chapter should really be more positive! Gender difference is really one of the great delights of being human. Years ago, my wife and I attended a Scottish wedding. At the reception, after the ceremony, everyone broke into folk dancing. Young and old, boys and girls, we did the Reel, 'ceilidh' dancing, and highland step-dancing to the music of the pipes and fiddle and accordion. Some of the steps were rather involved. I asked a young woman how it was that all the guests knew how to do each one of these dances, and she replied that they were taught in school. I thought to myself, now there is a truly advanced civilization! What was utterly marvelous was to see the men's and women's roles so clearly defined, yet so clearly harmonious.

God means for us to enjoy this unity within the diversity and diversity within the unity of the sexes.

So very sad that there is such confusion today. The gospel can heal this area as it can every other.

Discussion Questions:

1. Why have sexuality and gender distinctions become a battlefield, rather than a place for genuine discussion?

2. Have Christians, or the church, been overly harsh in their treatment of gay people or people of alternative sexual orientations?

3. How may we be more persuasive and not just apply the letter of the law to those with whom we disagree?

4. How may we defend the civil rights of people who are outside of biblical patterns for sexuality, but yet are still human beings made after God's image?

Has Darwin Refuted Genesis?

IGNORANCE MORE FREQUENTLY BEGETS CONFIDENCE THAN DOES KNOWLEDGE: IT IS THOSE WHO KNOW LITTLE, AND NOT THOSE WHO KNOW MUCH, WHO SO POSITIVELY ASSERT THAT THIS OR THAT PROBLEM WILL NEVER BE SOLVED BY SCIENCE (CHARLES DARWIN).

Like many young boys I wanted to be a scientist when I grew up. As a teenager I came under the sway of a couple of the science teachers at our boarding school. They somehow made such things as chemical experiments, star-gazing, and measuring the depths of the ocean as exciting as could be. Our school had an arrangement with the famous Woods Hole Oceanographic Institute on Cape Cod, and we would go there and join the scientists in their quests better to understand the world under the sea. When I first learned about the theory of evolution it was through an American playwright turned

93

scientist whose books, African Genesis (1961) and The Territorial Imperative (1966) were compelling to my young mind. Along with Raymond Dart and Konrad Lorenz, Robert Ardrey became the articulate proponent of territoriality and the killer ape theory, which held that man's early ancestors were warlike, and that in order to understand modern humanity we would have to realize his natural aggressiveness. This was wonderful stuff for a young boy growing up in the Cold War years. Most of his theories have been disproved, yet there was something about his Darwinian sense of survival of the fittest that appealed to many at the time. Why do we go to war? It's in our background! Though entirely secular this diagnosis is not altogether foreign to our Christian anthropology. We are indeed by nature warlike. And it did begin with one of our ancestors!

Still, the widely-held belief in human evolution is troubling for Christians. Charles Darwin, author of the powerful book, On the Origins of Species (1859), taught that we came about through survival of the fittest. If you read the early chapters of Genesis straightforwardly they do not appear to portray a world of predators and survivors. So, must we simply accept a conflict between evolutionary theory and any biblical account? Must we even stay shy of biological or paleontological science? No, because an honest look at both the Bible and the history of science shows far less of a mismatch than might be supposed. A heavy dose of patience and modesty have helped me develop a quiet confidence that the God who made the world is the same God who wrote the Bible. I certainly do not have all the answers. But I am relatively optimistic about resolving the supposed conflict between religion and science, and if not, at least being able to respect both, and not feel threatened by either.

How We Found Ourselves at War

FOR IF THIS PLAN OR THIS UNDERSTANDING IS OF MAN, IT WILL FAIL; BUT IF IT IS OF GOD YOU WILL NOT BE ABLE TO OVERTHROW THEM. YOU MIGHT EVEN BE FOUND OPPOSING GOD! (ACTS 5:38-39)

The first question to ask when discussing the subject of biblical faith and science is why so many people perceive there is a conflict. One of the images that feeds this perception is the famous Scopes trial of 1925. What most people remember about the trial was that 'fundamentalism' was ridiculed by the more enlightened modern mentality. This is particularly true if the only acquaintance one has with the case is through the Hollywood movie Inherit the Wind, starring Spencer Tracy. The facts, as is often the case, tell a different story. John T. Scopes was a substitute teacher in the Tennessee school system, who was accused of presenting evolutionary theory in violation of the state's law prohibiting the teaching of human evolution in any state-funded school. Though in the end Scopes was found guilty, fined $100, a verdict which was overturned on a technicality, the reason the case got such notoriety is that it all became the center of high drama, broadcast on the radio and reported by every major newspaper. The great Presbyterian populist politician William Jennings Bryan argued for the prosecution, and the notorious atheist Clarence Darrow for the defense. One of the journalists who descended on the city was the well-known skeptic, H. L. Mencken, representing the Baltimore Sun. He branded it the 'Monkey Trial,' a label that stuck through the ensuing decades. (Curiously, the science textbook required by Tennessee law contained teachings on evolution, so that in effect teachers had to violate the law!) Strictly speaking the case was about whether or not the young teacher had broken the law, in fact what was most often debated was the credibility of Scripture. Darrow put Bryan on the stand and pressed him on such issues as where did Cain find a wife, and how could Eve have been made from Adam's rib, and how Jonah could have lived in the belly of a great fish – standard questions, often asked, and which have perfectly good answers. But it made Christians look bad.

Other debates about evolution had gone before, often with the same combination of fact and mythology. One of the most famous was between Bishop Samuel Wilberforce and Thomas Huxley, sometimes known as 'Darwin's bulldog'. The debate took place at the Oxford University Museum, June 30th, 1860, shortly after the publication of one of Darwin's explosive books. Like the Scopes trial this debate is remembered for its bluster more than for its substance. Wilberforce apparently asked Huxley whether it was through his grandfather or grandmother that he was descended from a monkey. To which Huxley is meant to have answered he'd rather be related to an ape than to a bigot who obscured the truth. And like the later Scopes conflict this debate was characterized as a pitched battle between religion and science, whereas in fact it was more of a conflict between liberal and conservative Anglicans (the liberal Anglicans were open to Darwin's theories). Indeed, many opponents of Darwin's theory were well respected scientists, and by no means largely clergy.

So, it is only fair to ask what really happened, to give the popular impression that religion and science are at loggerheads? In a word, the Enlightenment of the eighteenth century.[1] When we look at the historical record we find a few surprises awaiting us. The first is that modern science was largely developed by believing Christians. People such as Nicolaus Copernicus (1473-1543), Johannes Kepler (1571-1630), Galileo Galilei (1564-1642), and the great Isaac Newton (1643-1727) were Christians of various stripes, who all wanted to verify the order in the universe as God had created it. The so-called scientific method, the way of verifying hypotheses by repetition of experiments, was invented by Francis Bacon (1561-1626) by using experiments to eliminate alternative theories. But then came a gradual shift in mentalities. To put it succinctly, but fairly, the great claim of Enlightenment thought was that God seemed less and less necessary as the ultimate cause of the world, because human reason was sufficient to discover all of life's patterns.

Perhaps the most central assertion made by leading thinkers of the Enlightenment was that the church has been holding humanity back from its full potential. The quintessential Enlightenment

1. K. Scott Oliphint sets forth this history in his excellent book, Know Why You Believe, Grand Rapids: Zondervan, 2017, pp. 152-159.

philosopher Immanuel Kant said this eloquently in his essay, What Is Enlightenment? (1784) when he declared that now humanity would be released from its immaturity. The key sentence is this: 'immaturity is the inability to use one's own understanding without the guidance of another.'[2] To put it simply, the core conviction of the Enlightenment was that we do not need to depend on the authority of any one or any institution in the search for truth. Whatever may be the facts, the impression was given that religion, instead of being the promoter of scientific inquiry that it had been, was now its opponent.[3]

Eventually a conflict developed and it was assumed by many that the terms of the conflict were right. But they simply are not. What we have on the one side is a worldview which confuses scientific discoveries with absolute truth. And the other side which at its best was the biblical world and life view. Mary Midgley, in the book Evolution as a Religion, argues that Darwinists often made Darwin's thought far

---

2. Kant: Political Writings, ed. H. S. Reiss, transl. H. B. Nisbet, 2nd, enlarged edition, Cambridge: Cambridge University Press, 1991, p. 54.

3. Books began to be written such as J. W. Draper, History of the Conflict between Religion and Science (1874) and A. D. White, A History of the Warfare of Science with Theology in Christendom (1896). I own these two books and it is striking how superficial they are.

more radical than he intended it, and turned much of evolutionary theory into a religion.[4] As far as I know Midgley is not a professing Christian. However, her critique of much modern science has taken on messianic zeal. She is equally critical of religion promoting bad science. Her goal is to celebrate the greatest scientists, such as Theodosius Dobzhansky, Albert Einstein and others who remind us of how small scientific achievement is, compared to what there is to know.

Are Christians Always Helpful?

BE NOT RASH WITH YOUR MOUTH, NOR LET YOUR HEART BE HASTY TO UTTER WORDS BEFORE GOD, FOR GOD IS IN HEAVEN AND YOU ARE ON EARTH (ECCLESIASTES 5:2).

It is only fair to ask, were believers simply misunderstood victims, or forgotten heroes? To be sure there have been all along remarkable scientists who are also people of faith. When I was a student at Harvard University there was a professor of astronomy and of the history of science who was a practicing Christian. Owen Gingerich, among his many achievements, contributed to a better understanding of the nature of the planets, to a

---

4. Mary Midgley, Evolution as a Religion: Strange Hopes and Stranger Fears, London: Metnhuen, 1985.

defense of Copernicus' writings, and even has an asteroid named after him. Another remarkable scientist who is a Christian is Francis Collins, who is considered one of the greatest 'gene hunters' of all time. After the discovery of the human genome, he declared that the experience was deeply humbling because he had caught the first glimpse of our own instruction book, known hitherto only by God. Both men have written on the compatibility between science and the Christian faith.[5] And there are a host of others.

But there have also been Christians who have given the faith a bad name. They have tried to use the Bible as a scientific textbook, which it was not intended to be. Certainly, when the Scriptures speak of the creation or of historical data, they speak authoritatively. But they are not a manual for science. Here is an example of what I believe to be a misguided use of the Bible. According to some, the second law of thermodynamics has its origins in Genesis 3. This law says something like

5. Francis Collins, *The Language of God: A Scientist Presents Evidence for Belief,* New York: The Free Press, 2006. Both Gingerich and Collins would call themselves 'theistic evolutionists,' a position not endorsed by every Christian. By 'evolution' it is important to note they are not defending Darwin's theories, but simply that the creation may have taken a long period of time.

this: whenever energy is transferred an increasing amount of it is wasted and cannot be reused. There is thus increasing entropy or disorder in the system. A popular way of putting this law is, you cannot unscramble an egg. This is the result, according to some very conservative Christians, of the fall of man, recorded in the Book of Genesis.

Real Questions, Adequate Answers
WHERE WERE YOU WHEN I LAID THE FOUNDATIONS OF THE EARTH? (JOB 38:4)

So, where must we go next? One place is to question the legitimacy of the Enlightenment. Not all of it, of course, but its claims for the capacity of unaided human reason to understand everything, even when it contradicts revelation. But another is to find the proper excitement about doing science shared by its originators. I believe my schoolboy enthusiasm was right. Science has not only given us so many modern comforts and medical advances, but also a sense of great wonder. I don't want to lose that. To preserve that sense we need to be the best observers of the world. There is so much to explore! We need to find ways to promote human flourishing through the best science. But we also need to ask honest questions. Even if Darwinism is wrong as a worldview, does the

Bible allow us to believe in a longer period of time for the creation of the world? Is some degree of violence in nature compatible with the pre-fallen world? What are permissible and what are impermissible types of genetic engineering? Where do dinosaurs fit in? How did the world become populated as rapidly as it did, according to Genesis? Or did it? How did races develop? How can we protect the earth's ecosystems without becoming pantheists?

These should not be seen as threats but as great opportunities to discover the wonder of how God made the world. And that should lead us to worship him all the more.

Discussion Questions:

1. If modern science was largely developed by Christians what happened for there to be such conflict between biblical faith and science?

2. Is evolutionary theory a religion?

3. How should human reason be used as a legitimate tool for understanding the way the universe functions?

How Hard are Questions from Muslims?

WE NEED TO ASK OURSELVES, WHAT ARE MUSLIMS LONGING FOR? WHAT KEEPS MUSLIMS FROM ATTAINING THIS? (J. T. SMITH)

This final chapter may come as a surprise. Why single out Islam, and why listen to the challenges they issue? It is the fastest-growing religion, other than the Christian faith, in the world. More and more towns are populated by Muslims. And, of course, we hear almost daily in the news about Islamists, who, the majority of Muslims believe, do not represent the true faith, even though they use some of its concepts.

My own church participates in 'meetings for better understanding' with the local mosque. It has been quite a learning experience for both sides. Some of the objections we have heard from our Muslim friends are quite surprising, unanticipated. It is the same for them as they listen to us. On one day the subject was Adam. For Christians who take the Bible seriously he was a real person, and the head of the human race by way of the covenant. When he and Eve succumbed to the serpent's temptation it infected the entire human race after them. Jesus Christ came as the last Adam, the Second Man (1 Corinthians 15:45-48), heading up redeemed humanity in a new covenant by repairing the first Adam's transgression. The Muslim imam then replied. Adam was the first Muslim. His sin was not particularly serious. In fact, the imam declared, Allah loves it when people sin, because he loves showing them forgiveness. Adam simply 'stumbled' he told us, and that provides a great encouragement to the rest of us who are prone to moral weakness.

This rather low view of transgression is confirmed by what I have learned over the years: there is an official Islam, which includes a number of basics, and then there is a folk Islam. According to official Islam there are five pillars of true faith: (1) the testimony of faith (one must be able to say, 'there is no god but Allah, and Muhammad is his prophet; (2) one must pray five times a day, facing Mecca; (3) it is required to give alms for the poor; (4) one must fast during the month of Ramadan (a lunar month); and (5) if possible, a male Muslim must go on pilgrimage at least once to Mecca. However, in folk Islam all kinds of practices and beliefs are not specified in the Qur'an or the Hadith. For example, many Muslims believe in the Jinn. These beings, from which we get the word genie, do appear in the Qur'an. They are evil spirits who can disguise themselves into different forms. A friend of mine was having tea with a Muslim business student in Philadelphia. He was in every respect a Westernized person. When they had finished the tea, my friend started to pour the remaining hot water down the sink. 'Stop!' ordered the student. 'You'll disturb the Jinn.'

The lack of seriousness of sin belongs to the folk religion rather than official doctrine. Yet, it is believed by large numbers of Muslims. For example, it is considered understandable that a man is perfectly justified to lust after a woman. Even adultery is not as serious as it is, for example, in the Christian religion. Male weaknesses, such as promiscuous sexual desire, are considered normal and easily forgivable. This sort of view is in contrast to the impression most outsiders have that Islam is a terribly strict, legalistic religion. Of course, it can be, depending on where and by whom it is being practiced. Sharia law is a body of legal ordinances which cover all of life. But different countries practice different parts of the law books. For example, there is no uniform teaching on women wearing the Burqa. But in some countries it is expected. Others are more free.

What Muslims Think of the Gospel

BY THIS ALL PEOPLE WILL KNOW THAT YOU ARE MY DISCIPLES, IF YOU HAVE LOVE FOR ONE ANOTHER (JOHN 13:35).

I have always found it important to put my feet into other people's shoes. So, it is important to ask, how do Muslims feel about us? Some of what follows may come as a surprise. But unless we have some idea of how our Muslim neighbor perceives Christian people, we will be ineffective in approaching them. Here are four issues that have impressed themselves on me, mostly from conversations I've held with Islamic people.

1. One of the common views held by Muslims is that the West is a Christian civilization. They often wonder how it is that there is so much decadence in the West. Why do people dress immodestly? How can we celebrate the likes of Madonna and Lady Gaga? Why is there nudity in films? They often make the connection: Christianity equals decadence. Answering this

requires some degree of sophistication. There is a connection between the Christian faith and some of Western civilization. Shakespeare, Bach, Rembrandt, and so many others would make no sense were it not for the influence of the Christian message. But, as we saw in the case of the supposed warfare between science and faith another factor intervened which stands in conscious opposition to the Christian faith, namely the Enlightenment. Thus, as the West modernized, while there certainly remained some Christian influence, the Enlightenment mentality, with its faith in unaided human reason, intervened. We must ask our friends to look carefully at the difference, and not blame the Christian message for all the excesses of modern culture.

2. Another question Muslims often ask is whether Christians want to take over the world. Their reasoning is that Jesus told his followers to go into all the world and make disciples. Also, a certain amount of modern history appears to be driven by the Christian desire to colonize. Indeed, during the nineteenth century there were great commercial powers, such as the Dutch, the

British, the French, who in different ways tried to have the support of Christians, whether they were missionaries or simply traders, to help with their ascendancy. Sometimes too Muslims will hear the word 'crusade', which carries a negative connotation for them. For example, when an American president talked about conducting a crusade against terror, he thought it was an innocent use of a word. But to a Muslim the word signifies the holy warfare against them in the twelfth and thirteenth centuries directed by the pope. Again, some of this is plausible, but is mostly based on profound misunderstandings. To make disciples in the New Testament sense is not a call to world conquest, but to faith in Jesus Christ. It is actually Islam that has inbuilt theocratic tendencies, whereas the Christian faith supports social pluralism, as well as an appropriate distinction between the church and the state. It might be wise for Christians to refrain from using a loaded word like 'crusade,' even though those medieval wars are greatly misunderstood by modern people. Of course, we would like to see more people coming to a saving knowledge of the Lord, but this is worlds away from some sort of takeover.

3. A third common perception is that all Christians support Israel and not the Palestinians. This seems quite unfair and cannot help but tar Christians as unjust, and ignorant of history. This is actually an important issue for Christians to get straight. Much of European and North American support for Israel comes from two concerns, one quite legitimate and the other less so. Legitimately, the free West had an enormous concern for the Jewish victims of the Holocaust during World War II. One way to help, they often thought, was to support the newly founded state of Israel under the leadership of David Ben-Gurion, and supported by American President Harry S. Truman. The story is rather romantically told in Leon Uris' The Exodus, which was made into a block-buster movie directed by Otto Preminger. The second reason is that a number of conservative Christians believe that in the end times the Jews will return in great numbers to Israel. Their view is based on a rather literal interpretation of a number of Old Testament prophecies, such as the future restoration of Israel predicted by Ezekiel, which centers on the rebuilding of the temple (Ezekiel 40-48). There is legitimate

debate about what these chapters mean. Many Christians believe the rebuilt temple is a spiritual one, beginning with Jesus' resurrection and continuing to the construction of the Christian church (John 2:19; Ephesians 2:19-22). Chapters nine, ten and eleven of Romans contains the phrase, 'And in this way all Israel will be saved' (Romans 11:26). But the context makes it clear that this cannot mean literally every single Jewish person. Indeed, Paul argues strenuously that there is only one way for all people, Jews and Gentiles alike, to be saved, and that is through faith in Jesus Christ. But the former view has blinded some Christians to the social justice issues between modern Israel and Palestine.

4. Some of the questions posed by Muslims are more theological. For example, how could God have a son? He would have to marry, and this is utterly unthinkable. Here we need to help our friends understand the doctrine of the Trinity. It is admittedly a high mystery. How can there be one God who is in three Persons? We don't fully understand, but it is a crucial part of what we believe. When Muslims hear about the Trinity they think Christians must be polytheists,

believing in several gods. But we insist that there is one God who exists nevertheless in three Persons. Each of the Persons is fully God and participates in the creation and in redemption in distinctive ways: the Father plans it all, the Son executes it (by becoming man) and the Holy Spirit applies it (see 2 Corinthians 13:14). And unless Jesus was crucified we will die in our sins. Muslims cannot accept letting a great prophet, as they believe he was, die. Our God, as we said earlier, has wounds.

I think in the end the great difference in our two faiths is that the God of the Bible so loved the world that he gave his Son so that whoever believes in him may not die but have everlasting life (John 3:16). Muslims believe that Allah has ninety-nine names. But none of them is love. He is called the all-merciful one, but that is not quite the same. In my conversations with Muslim friends the one constant I have found is that he or she does not have real assurance of God's personal love for them. But we can. John tells us we may have confidence, and not shrink from him in shame at his coming (1 John 2:38). May all who read these lines find such a confidence in the God who has loved sinners from all eternity.

Discussion Questions:

1. What is the relative importance of right doctrine and right practice when reaching out to Muslims?

2. What are some concrete ways we may reach out to Muslims as people, rather than as terrorists?

3. Is Islam at the root a religion of violence?

How to Change the World?

EITHER WE CONFORM OUR DESIRES TO THE TRUTH OR WE CONFORM THE TRUTH TO OUR DESIRES (OS GUINNESS).

Most young people are idealistic. They want to make a difference. I am impressed with the current generation's concern for social justice issues. In my day we cared passionately about civil rights. Today many teenagers have a more global interest. This is not surprising since our world has shrunk, as it were. One of the issues on many a young person's agenda is international slavery. The statistics about this problem are quite appalling. About two million children are exploited every year for purposes of exploitation. Six in ten survivors testify that they were forced into prostitution. Ninety-eight per cent of the victims are women and girls.[1] There

---

1. See [https://www.equalitynow.org/traffickingFAQ]

are a number of excellent initiatives which deal with this area. One of them is the International Justice Mission (IJM), mentioned in chapter six. This is a global organization that aims to protect the poor from violence, particularly in the developing world. It is a Christian organization which tries to penetrate countries where justice is not working and where crime is rampant. Just to cite one example of their findings: in India there are literally millions of poor people held illegally in forced labor. Yet IJM can only identify five criminals who have done substantial prison time for trafficking in the last few years.[2]

The problem of international trafficking is only one of many that confront us today. The list of challenges is extensive. We might think of racism, poverty, exploitation of the environment, corruption in business and politics, pornography, terrorism, persecution of believers, deficient education, diseases of all kinds, and much more. In addition, there are social conflicts, personal psychological problems, marital fights, and the like. One is tempted to think nothing can be done to match the scale of these problems.

---

2. See [https://www.ijm.org/how-we-work]. Founder Gary A. Haugen has written a number of books and articles on their work. See his The Locust Effect: Why the End of Poverty Requires the End of Violence, Oxford, New York: Oxford University Press, 2015.

Christians have struggled to find the right way to react to the enormous problems we face. One of the most prevalent is to concentrate on the church and hope that the larger problems will take care of themselves once the Christian community is straightened out. This approach is typical of Anabaptist theology. Originally the Anabaptists wanted to restore the church to what they imagined its New Testament purity was. They are pacifists, believing that Christians should not bear arms nor go to war. The church is meant to be populated by 'uncompelled' people whereas the state may use force when necessary. This approach has some merit. It rightly sees the church as the center for the worship of God. But it fails to recognize the whole of creation as both fallen and in need of redemption. Other spheres besides the church are legitimate parts of the world, and Christians should have no hesitation trying to engage them. One of them is government. If ministries such as IJM were Anabaptist they would not be able to press different governments into changing their ways. Furthermore, Christians ought to feel called to be in public service. We need more believers in every sphere, including the state.

Perhaps the opposite extreme from the Anabaptist one is known as Caesaropapism. When the emperor Constantine declared the Christian faith to be a legal one, in 313, through the Edit of Milan, an enormous change occurred in the ancient world. Among other things, the emperor's role was to enforce doctrine, get rid of heresy and help ensure the unity of the church. The crafting of doctrine was done by the bishops, but the emperor would henceforth enforce their decisions. Many versions of this approach, right up to the present, can be found. One modern movement known as Christian Reconstruction, believes the bulk of the law of Moses can successfully be applied to today's issues, in order to transform society into a Christian culture. This view suffers from not realizing that since the death and resurrection of Jesus Christ we are no longer in the Old Testament economy and must instead find principles to guide us in modern times. It is true that the Bible contains numerous values which are of lasting significance. But we no longer live in the land of Palestine, governed by principles of the Israelite civil code.

Our Calling

I THEREFORE, A PRISONER FOR THE LORD, URGE YOU TO WALK IN A MANNER WORTHY OF THE CALLING TO WHICH YOU HAVE BEEN CALLED (EPHESIANS 4:1).

Is there another way, besides Anabaptist withdrawal and Caesaropapist engagement? Yes, it is to follow the apostle Paul's admonition: 'Do not be conformed to this world, but be transformed by the renewal of your mind, that by testing you may discern what is the will of God, what is good and acceptable and perfect' (Romans 12:2). This may sound like a pious platitude. It is anything but. What the apostle is telling us here is that if our minds are renewed, rather than being conformed to the mold of the present age, real metamorphosis can occur. To what then, is the renewal directed? To discern God's good will. The older word is prove. The idea is to learn by experience ('by testing') what is God's will, and thus to learn how approved the will of God is. God's will can never fail or be lacking for the present problems. John Murray, in his magnificent commentary on the Book of Romans, says this: 'There is not a moment of life that the will of God does not command, no circumstance that it does not fill with meaning if we are responsive to the fullness of his revealed counsel for us.'[3]

This means we need to go out into the world and engage in its issues. This is a favorite biblical principle. The author of Hebrews tells us that spiritual maturity is achieved when those who aspire to it 'have their powers of discernment trained by constant practice to distinguish good from evil' (Hebrews 5:14). The

3. John Murray, *The Epistle to the Romans,* vol. 2, Grand Rapids: Eerdmans, 1965, p. 115.

expression 'trained' is a translation of the Greek gumnazo from which we get our word gymnasium. In other words, we cannot learn to engage the issues of life, let alone decide what is the right path to take, if we simply stay in our chairs or sit at our desks. We need to get out into the gymnasium of life and get tossed about. Are you called to be a politician? Then find a way to get elected and then mix it up with those who don't agree with you and see if you can't persuade them. Are you called to be an artist? Then learn your craft well and see how far you get in the often confused world of the arts. Are you called to be a husband? A wife? A parent? These noble vocations require biblical wisdom and training in a virtuous character, in order to relate well to your spouse or your children.

Reformation and Renewal

LET THE WORK ON THIS HOUSE OF GOD ALONE. LET THE GOVERNOR OF THE JEWS AND THE ELDERS OF THE JEWS REBUILD THIS HOUSE OF GOD ON ITS SITE(EZRA 6:7).

This is not to say that to change the world is limited to individual transformation, followed by a trickle-down effect on the rest of the world. One of the most remarkable passages from the prophets is found buried in Jeremiah (chapters 28-29). The people of Israel found themselves in exile because of their treacherous behavior. Their captors were the Babylonians and the ruler Nebuchadnezzar. One of the false prophets, Hananiah, had told the people Nebuchadnezzar's yoke would be broken in a couple of years, and that the people would return to their land in peace. But Jeremiah, the true prophet, didn't buy it. He knew that the people were in for a long captivity. Hananiah died because of his deceit. But then Jeremiah sent a letter from Jerusalem to the survivors in exile.

Its contents are, for some, quite counter-intuitive. It tells the exiles, on behalf of the Lord God, to build houses, to live in them, to plant gardens and live on the fruit. It tells them to continue taking spouses and having children. And then, the most astonishing command: 'But seek the welfare of the city where I have sent you into exile, and pray the Lord on its behalf, for in its welfare you will find your welfare' (Jeremiah 29:7). Packed into the statement, 'seek the welfare of the city' is an entire program for social reform. The word 'welfare' is the marvelous Hebrew word shalom. While most people know this as a friendly greeting, it is actually far more. The term means good in a great variety of ways. It can be aesthetic good, as in beauty. More often it is a suitable or moral good. It typically means wholeness or even healing. In a favorite verse, it means justice and kindness: 'He has told you, O man, what is good; and what does the Lord require of you but to do justice and to love kindness, and to walk humbly with your God' (Micah 6:8). In his great prayer at the dedication of the temple Solomon asked that God would 'hear in heaven and forgive the sin of your servants, your people Israel, when you teach them the good way (way of shalom) in which they should walk … (1 Kings 8:36).

So, we are to bring good to this world, even though in a sense we are living as exiles until the time of the great resurrection. A number of urban ministries have adopted these verses as themes for their work as they seek to do good in the city. One of the ministries I love best is the London City Mission. They have been working in the city for nearly two hundred years (which is an advantage over many ministries, since they have the trust and credibility often lacking in start-ups). They are on the front lines: taking the gospel to the least reached, the homeless, the prisoners, recent immigrants and marginal ethnic groups. They are gospel-driven, but they also help people connect with employment opportunities, churches, city officials, etc.

Of course, the cities of the world need more than missions to marginal people. They need to feel the impact of the gospel in the business world, in the media, the transportation networks, and so forth. And we mustn't forget the suburbs or the more rural areas. While the city is often the darling of modern missions, that must not obscure the fact that our entire planet should be our concern.

You and Your Calling

And whatever you do, in word or deed, do everything I the name of the Lord Jesus, giving thanks to God the Father through him. (Colossians 3:17)

It still may feel overwhelming to look at the world's challenges and realize how small we are. But there is great comfort in knowing that we are not alone. The task of meeting global challenges would be overwhelming were it not for the reality of our calling. Small groups, church deacons, NGOs (Non Governmental Organizations), each of these must respond to the particular calling the Lord has given them. In my own case it became obvious that my gifts, such as they are, have led me into teaching. I have taught both at the high school level and at the graduate level. I have also led in youth work, both Christian and outside the church. I am as aware as anyone of the limits of this profession. One of the great honors my wife and I have enjoyed is mentoring young people. We have tried to provide a haven for troubled youth, or just be models for young people growing up, much as we benefitted from models in our own day.

Teaching is but one of hundreds of legitimate and potentially fruitful endeavors. I recently went to a class reunion. Among the accomplishments of my classmates were the practice of law, farming, construction work, acting, and the military. Not all of my mates found their life's calling right away. There were disappointments, bumps along the road, setbacks. Christians should set for themselves the goal of pleasing the Lord in everything they do. One of the great high callings is expressed in Paul's famous words, 'So, whether you eat or drink, or whatever you do, do all to the glory of God' (1 Corinthians 10:31). Whether or not we are entirely successful in life, and very few are, the goal of giving glory to God is a worthy one. And notice he says that you can do that in the most mundane of activities. With fear and trembling, we long to hear the words, 'Well done, good and faithful servant. You have been faithful over a little; I will set you over much. Enter into the joy of your master' (Matthew 25:23). Or, perhaps, a more modest hope. When the seventy-two disciples returned exuberant over their mission, Jesus told them,

'Nevertheless, do not rejoice in this, that the spirits are subject to you, but rejoice that your names are written in heaven' (Luke 10:20). Modest? No, marvelous! Yes, we ought to do everything in our power to change the world. But not at the expense of our salvation.

Discussion Questions

1. How may we avoid the equal but opposite mistakes of Anabaptism (withdrawal) and Caesaropapism (church control over all of life)?

2. Why are Christians reluctant to get involved in the rough and tumble of life?

3. Are you surprised by Jeremiah's advice to the Jewish people in exile?

4. Is every good endeavor really good, really legitimate?

Conclusions

Many more issues could be raised. This book intends to give confidence to those who would defend the Christian faith in our time. While it does not provide exhaustive answers, it has outlined some of the broad principles that can be applied to a number of concerns we share. You will notice that we do not have a twelve-step method or five airtight proofs for the existence of God. Instead, we want to recommend wisdom as the most important approach to explaining the faith to those who do not believe. For that matter, commending the faith in this way is also convincing to those who already have faith, but feel they lack resources to navigate the questions raised in our day.

At the heart of this wisdom is our relationship with the Lord. We mentioned the Puritans' theme of playing before an 'audience of one.' The Book of Proverbs in the Bible tells us 'The fear of the Lord is the beginning of wisdom, and the knowledge of the Holy One is insight' (Proverbs 9:10). The word 'fear' when used this way does not mean terror or dread, but a healthy reverence. There is a proper sense of awe and respect before the living God, but there is also meant to be a kind of intimacy, a friendship with him. From this beginning place we can live all of life, including speaking well of the Christian faith.

The apostle Peter tells his readers 'in your hearts honor Christ the Lord as holy, always being prepared to make a defense to anyone who asks you for a reason for the hope that is in you; yet do it with gentleness and respect' (1 Peter 3:15). Regarding Christ as holy is a New Testament way of saying 'the fear of the Lord.' When we properly worship Jesus Christ in our hearts, we will begin to have the words to speak to our generation. Earlier in this same letter, Peter tells us that our purpose, one that flows out of our primary relationship, is to 'proclaim the excellencies of him who called you out of darkness into his marvelous light' (1 Peter 2:9). The term 'apologetics' is just a fancy way of describing our privilege to proclaim the excellencies of our God.

CHRISTIAN FOCUS PUBLICATIONS

Christian Focus · Christian Heritage · CF4K · Mentor

Christian Focus Publications publishes books for adults and children under its four main imprints: Christian Focus, CF4K, Mentor and Christian Heritage. Our books reflect our conviction that God's Word is reliable and Jesus is the way to know him, and live for ever with him.

Our children's publication list includes a Sunday school curriculum that covers pre-school to early teens, and puzzle and activity books. We also publish personal and family devotional titles, biographies and inspirational stories that children will love.

If you are looking for quality Bible teaching for children then we have an excellent range of Bible stories and age-specific theological books.

From pre-school board books to teenage apologetics, we have it covered!

Find us at our web page:
www.christianfocus.com

CF4·K